F
Money Special

A CONSUMER'S GUIDE TO
BUYING AND SELLING
A HOME

The Daily Telegraph

A
FAMILY
MONEY-GO-ROUND
SPECIAL

A CONSUMER'S GUIDE TO
BUYING AND SELLING
A HOME

DIANA WRIGHT

Published by Telegraph Publications,
Peterborough Court, At South Quay,
181 Marsh Wall, London E14 9SR

First published as *A Consumer's Guide to Mortgages* 1983

First edition 1985
Second edition 1986
Third edition 1986
Fourth edition 1987
Fifth edition 1987

Typeset by Michael Weintroub Graphics Ltd, Kenton, Harrow
Printed and bound in Great Britain by Biddles Limited, Guildford and King's Lynn

British Library Cataloguing in Publication Data
Wright, Diana
    A consumer's guide to buying and selling a home. – 5th ed.
1. House buying – England   2. House selling – England
I. Title
333.33'8'0942   HD1379

ISBN 0-86367-181-0

CONTENTS

CHAPTER 5. REPAYMENT MORTGAGES 59

CHAPTER 6. ENDOWMENT MORTGAGES 71

CHAPTER 7. PENSION MORTGAGES 85

CHAPTER 8. WHICH MORTGAGE TO CHOOSE? 97

ACKNOWLEDGEMENTS

Writing a book such as this requires an enormous supporting cast of individuals with specialist knowledge of one or another of the various fields connected with the whole process of house buying.

I would in particular like to thank solicitor Brenda Hatton, and many individuals from the Woolwich Building Society, London Life, Equitable Life, and the Building Societies Association, most of whom have had to put up with an almost never-ending stream of questions. Finally, the mortgage figures used here have been extracted with great patience by Steve Perry from the Nationwide Building Society's computer.

INTRODUCTION TO THE SERIES

A home is the most expensive thing most people ever buy – until they buy their next home. Any mistake can therefore be a very expensive one. Some people possibly spend as much on petrol, holidays or even on dining out as they do on their mortgage, but if they buy the wrong brand or visit the wrong place this time, it is money wasted only once: next time there is the opportunity to make a better choice. Buy the wrong house or a property in the wrong place – or finance the acquisition in the wrong manner – and the mistake may still be being paid for in decades to come.

Few can afford to make mistakes, but housebuying and selling is not an area in which many are well experienced. Even at the end of a lifetime the typical person will have moved little more than half a dozen times at the most, and the first-time buyer has no first-hand experience at all. Even the experienced mover will find that things change as he moves from flat to house, leasehold to freehold, registered to unregistered property. Even switching between North and South produces differences in estate agency and other practices, and the choice of mortgages available now is very different from what was on offer even five years ago.

The value of obtaining a life-assurance policy in connection with the mortgage – or now a pension policy – is very likely to have changed too, so even the lessons learned before may not answer today's problems.

Housebuying has changed considerably, and it remains as complex for the new buyer or the seasoned home-mover. There are plenty of people willing to offer advice – but most have a vested interest, even though it is not always evident. The life-assurance salesman clearly has an interest in persuading the buyer to take an endowment rather than a repayment mortgage: it is his living. But not all new buyers realise that the building society or bank manager can have the same incentive to suggest a loan repaid through a policy, because they too receive commission on the other companies' policies they sell. Or, they may offer no choice of policy at all: only their own. Solicitors and estate agents too earn part of their living from arranging insurance on behalf of housebuyers.

It is thus to books such as this that the innocent buyer has to turn for independent advice. It is one of a series published by *The Daily Telegraph*. The newspaper itself in its twice-weekly

Money-Go-Round section gives regular advice on housebuying matters, detailing the changes which take place in financing, conveyancing or surveying practices. It is the broadest and most comprehensive selection of articles printed in any national newspaper, but while its pages can give regular updating, it requires a book such as this to concentrate all the information into one readily accessible source which can go into greater detail than a newspaper possibly can.

Such is the speed at which practices in the housebuying market have changed since this book was first published that the author has had to update it for this new edition. It remains a book which can be read from cover to cover by those interested in all aspects of house buying and selling or dipped into by those with a particular problem to solve, or who simply want clarification of what they are being told by others. Like the rest of the books in this series, it is not intended to make readers into experts in subjects which they may encounter only occasionally: the aim is to provide the help of experts when it is required. This book meets that objective admirably.

Richard Northedge
Deputy City Editor
The Daily Telegraph

AUTHOR'S PREFACE

Four years ago, almost to the day, I was writing the final chapters of this book, and moving house. Both wheels have come full circle and a new edition of the book will just about coincide with another house move. These four years have seen major changes in the house-buying scene, which my own experience has reflected.

Four years ago, I remember, there was no point shopping around estate agents. They all charged 2 per cent for a sole agency, 2½ per cent for shared. (This was in London.) This time round, it's hardly an exaggeration to say they were beating a path to my door, offering to take it on for anything from 1 per cent upwards.

Stamp duty, in those days, was an unpalatable 2 per cent, but at least it only started at £30,000, which then meant lots of first time buyers escaped scot-free, and there were plenty of hints on how to bring the purchase price below that magic figure (you pretend the balance relates to fixtures and fittings, basically). Today, that sort of article would bring a hollow laugh in great swathes of the country, particularly in London and the South East. The limit has remained at £30,000, though thank goodness the rate of duty has been halved, to 1 per cent.

The first edition of the book had a throwaway line, somewhere, to the effect that wherever 'building society' was mentioned, it did, of course, also mean other mortgage lenders such as the banks. It didn't seem all that important then; a few people, it was true, went to their bank for a mortgage, but the vast bulk of lending then was in the hands of the societies, and many were slightly suspicious of the banks who had jumped into mortgage lending with a great fanfare a couple of years previously, only to withdraw shortly afterwards as they ran out of funds.

No, if you wanted a mortgage in those days, unquestionably the first place you would go to was 'your' building society, and if you'd saved a tidy sum, and you were lucky enough not to have hit on one of the periodic 'mortgage famines' then you'd be rewarded accordingly with a nice mortgage – for which you said 'thank you'.

If you weren't so lucky, or you hadn't been so prudent in your savings, you went off to a mortgage broker, and for the price of getting an endowment mortgage (an expensive decision in those days, as everyone charged you an extra ½ per cent on the loan for endowments) he would open the doors to finance. You might have decided to go to a broker anyway, if you were borrowing a large amount, to guide you through the labyrinth of differential rates for larger loans. While all the lenders charged the same basic mortgage rate, the pattern of differential rates was incredibly confusing and always changing. If you were looking for £50,000 in those days, you could have found yourself paying up to 2 per cent over the basic rate.

It's hard to believe, but it was only four years ago that most people were still making their mortgage payments gross, and getting tax relief through their PAYE codings. If you were moving house that year, you suddenly found your new mortgage was on the 'MIRAS' system (standing for Mortgage Interest Relief at Source), meaning much lower payments in terms of the figures you fill in on the monthly standing order or direct debit, though of course little change overall, as your net pay also falls to compensate. In fact, as basic rate tax has fallen in two successive budgets, people have had to get used to their mortgage payments going *up,* as the tax relief falls.

Not all these aspects have changed completely. Building societies are still the dominant force in house lending, and are expected to remain so for quite some time. But the balance has still swung significantly: this year, it is estimated that the banks and specialist new mortgage lenders are taking a 30 per cent share of new lending, and thanks to this competition, it seems, mortgage famines are genuinely gone for good.

The competition has been good for borrowers in other ways too: the ½ per cent differential on endowment mortgages has been abolished, and gone also are the higher rates for larger loans. But there's no longer complete unanimity on what the basic mortgage rate is at any one time, and there are fixed rate offers or such delights as 'cap and collar' mortgages to ponder as well.

The borrowers may still be hot footing it round to the mortgage broker, not to prise open the door to money, but to seek advice on which door in a well populated street he should go and knock.

Other aspects of moving house, sad to say, remain much the same: those weeks or months of nail biting until contracts are finally exchanged; the tales of gazumping and other dirty

dealings; the quaint command of English possessed by many estate agents that renders a run down wreck as ripe for improvement or a pest ridden backyard as a spacious patio.

Ah well, it's all part of the game. Despite all the problems and all the irritations, thousands of people manage to complete the process every year. I hope this book makes it that bit easier.

July 1987   Diana Wright

CHAPTER 1

HOME-BUYING FOR BEGINNERS

Buying a home, most people will tell you, is the biggest single investment you will ever make. It is certainly likely to be the biggest purchase that you will ever make; whether it turns out to be an investment in the sense that it will reward you with an increasing real value, so that you will make a decent profit when you sell, is another matter.

At any rate, for most people, buying a place to live in – as opposed to renting one, or sharing accommodation with parents – is the most sensible and often the only possible option to take.

THE INCREASE IN OWNER-OCCUPATION

The growth in 'owner-occupied' property in this country has been steadily increasing over the century. In 1914 just over 10 per cent of all dwellings were owner-occupied; by the end of the last war, the proportion had risen to a quarter. In 1970 we passed the half-way mark, and since then the proportion has been inching steadily upwards, so that, today, more than 60 per cent of all properties were bought (or in the process of being bought) by their occupiers.

This growth has taken place almost exclusively at the expense of the privately rented sector, which has shrunk from around 30 per cent of the total in 1960 to around 10 per cent today, while council house sales have also helped to swell the ranks of owner-occupiers.

There have been various reasons for this: one of the main ones, curiously enough, has been inflation. If there was no inflation at all, there would be little to choose, in monetary terms, between renting and buying.

Assuming that you have to borrow the money to buy your house, if there was 'zero' inflation' it would work out more expensive to buy than to rent, because you would be paying capital back as well as interest on the money you borrowed. If you are renting, on the other hand, you are effectively only paying 'interest' to the owner of the property, who has the option of selling the house and investing his realised capital, say, in a deposit account that pays interest.

There are, of course, all sorts of reasons why this theory does not work in practice. Landlords may be greedy and seek more rent from their property than it actually deserves; they may decide at a moment's notice to sell the house, so that the tenant is out on the street with no warning; or it may be difficult to force the landlord to keep his side of the bargain, which is to maintain the property in a decent state of repair. All of these proved very real problems, and the Government stepped in with the 1974 Rent Act, which gave a measure of protection to tenants.

This in itself accelerated the decline in privately rented property because, broadly speaking, it shifted the whole advantage from the landlord to the tenant, even if they were not paying an economic rent. Renting out property was no longer a sensible investment policy to pursue.

The supply of rented property was not only diminishing, but at the same time the positive advantage of owning (or buying) a property as opposed to renting one was also increasing. And this is where inflation comes in.

THE EFFECTS OF INFLATION

Buying a property, as far as most people are concerned, entails borrowing the money to do so. At times of high inflation, it is an excellent idea to buy a property, the value of which is probably increasing at least in line with inflation, by means of a fixed loan. The technical term used here is 'gearing'. If you borrow £18,000 to buy a house costing £20,000, for example, and supposing it appreciates by say 20 per cent a year for the next three years, it will be worth £34,560 at the end of that time – that is £14,560 profit for the £2,000 put down.

Obviously, you will have been paying interest on the loan in the meantime (and possibly repaying a bit of capital), but when you consider that the mortgage payments were probably little more than a comparable rent, you have without doubt made a very shrewd investment of that £2,000.

Some observers maintain that the 'profits' that house-buyers make on their property are illusory – after all, when they move, they will find that anywhere else they want to buy will be just as expensive. That is not strictly true. There are plenty of people today – not excessively well off – who are living in houses worth £50,000 or £100,000 with a mortgage of just £25,000. They have not needed to borrow more money because of the profits made on their previous property and therefore they have genuinely benefited – it is not simply a matter of 'paper profits'.

Inflation has in many ways been kind to owner-occupiers. Table 1 shows how house prices have risen since 1970. It can be seen that there have been two great 'leaps' – the first in 1972 to 1974 and the second in 1978 to 1980. In between these surges, however, there have been slack periods where prices on the whole have risen more slowly than the rate of inflation. Buyers who have benefited most are those who have timed their purchase just before one of the periodic jumps in house prices.

Table 1 Average house prices since 1970

Year	£
1970	5,000
1971	5,650
1972	7,420
1973	10,020
1974	11,100
1975	11,945
1976	12,759
1977	13,712
1978	15,674
1979	20,143
1980	23,514
1981	24,503
1982	24,577
1983	27,192
1984	29,648
1985	31,876
1986	38,000

Source: *Building Societies Association and Department of the Environment.*

However, people do not always move house simply because the general economic circumstances look good. Around a million people buy property every year, and the majority of these are probably due to circumstances such as marriage, moving to a different area for job reasons, moving after retirement and so on.

Today, we do not have the big helping hand from high inflation rates that benefited buyers in the 1970s. All the same, even at the current 'low' inflation rates, inflation can help to transform the real amount we are paying out on the mortgage, given time. Table 2 shows how the real value of a fixed payment of £100 diminishes according to various inflation rates.

What the table assumes is that payments will remain fixed in monetary terms. This is not to be relied on, of course: although the capital borrowed remains fixed, the interest rate does not.

In the last few years, interest rates have gone up and down like a yo-yo, with an average of three changes a year. In 1986, rates went from 13 per cent in January to 12.25 per cent in April, and then down to 11 per cent in May, and up to 12.25 per cent in October to fall by 1 per cent in May 1987. It was only in 1984 that we had the happy experience (for a few months!) of a mortgage rate of 10.25 per cent. Looking simply at the figures, though, only tells one side of the story. For the last couple of years, we have also experienced a steadily reducing rate of inflation which, however much it might benefit us in other ways, is bad news for the borrower.

A mortgage rate of 15 per cent gross, when inflation is also in double figures, is actually 'cheaper' money than borrowing at 12 per cent when inflation is less than 5 per cent and still falling. That said, as far as the borrower is concerned, it is not price inflation that matters but wage inflation. And wage inflation is – for those of us lucky enough to be in work – running at a consistently higher rate than the rise in prices.

Table 2 'Real' value of a fixed £100 payment at various rates of inflation

Year	4%	5%	6%	7%	8%
1	96.15	95.23	94.33	93.45	92.59
2	92.45	90.70	88.99	87.34	85.73
3	88.89	86.38	83.96	81.62	79.38
4	85.48	82.27	79.20	76.28	73.50
5	82.19	78.35	74.72	71.29	68.05
10	67.55	61.39	55.83	50.83	46.31
20	45.63	37.68	31.18	25.84	21.45
25	37.51	29.53	23.29	18.42	14.60

It is probably this factor which explains the continuing rise in house prices, over and above inflation – despite the expense of money, and despite the high percentage of unemployed. All the same, it is worth remembering that the days of the 1970s, when mortgage rates were cocooned from market forces – thanks partly to the 'cartel' of the Building Societies Association – have now gone for good. We are now paying a higher price for our mortgages than we were a decade ago.

CONCESSIONS TO HOME-BUYERS

There are still a couple of bright spots in the home-buying picture: successive Governments have all (so far) agreed that private ownership is a phenomenon to be encouraged, and the tax system contains some valuable benefits for home-buyers. The first is the concession whereby interest on loans for the purpose of house purchase qualifies for tax relief and the second is the exemption from capital gains tax of the profits made from selling your main home.

TAX RELIEF

This concession is limited to borrowers who are using the loan to buy their main residence (it is not allowed for second homes or holiday cottages) and it is limited to the first £30,000 of any loan.

This £30,000 limit looks paltry compared to what the house-buyer a decade ago was able to enjoy. In 1974, the limit for tax relief was £25,000 and the average house cost just over £11,000, in other words, less than half the limit. Today, the average house price throughout the UK has burst through the £30,000 barrier, standing at £38,000 on average in 1986, while in areas such as London and the rest of the South-East, it is beyond that, at around £50,000. If the limit is not raised, an increasing number of house-buyers are going to do without the safety net of tax relief on at least part of their mortgage. It has to be said that there is no immediate prospect of the limit being raised. On the contrary, all the speculation is centred on whether it will remain at all, or be abolished.

Most commentators think it unlikely that the relief will ever be withdrawn in one fell swoop: the 'death by a thousand cuts' is a much more politically acceptable alternative. In other words, the limit will be allowed to remain, but to become worth relatively less and less as house prices rise.

The position for higher-rate taxpayers is less certain, however. At the moment, relief is allowed against your highest rate of tax –

which means that the richer you are the more you benefit, not a principle which fits into a progressive system of taxation.

If we are laying odds on future changes in the system of giving tax relief to house-buyers, the withdrawal of higher-rate relief must be an obvious candidate – particularly if a Government of a more left-wing persuasion comes to power. Certainly the Labour party has hinted it will seriously consider doing so.

We have mentioned that the relief is available only to borrowers buying their principal residence. However, the relief is also extended to people who have to live in a place provided by their employment (caretakers are an obvious example); they are allowed to buy a separate home of their own – for retirement, perhaps. You may also benefit from the relief if you are buying the property for an 'elderly or infirm' relative, or for your divorced spouse. All this, however, counts towards the single limit of £30,000: you do not get two or three lots according to how many places you are buying.

As with other aspects of the tax system, the rules on tax relief actually discriminate against married couples. Single people are allowed a limit of £30,000 each; married couples have to make do with one between them.

EXEMPTION FROM CAPITAL GAINS TAX

Again, this concession – the exemption from capital gains tax on the profits made from selling your main residence – does not apply to profits made on selling a second home or a holiday cottage. Even if the concession were ever to be withdrawn (which seems unlikely), home-buyers now are not likely to be hit too hard by the tax, as there are other provisions to exempt 'inflation only' gains.

MORTGAGE INTEREST RELIEF AT SOURCE

Some years ago, the Government brought in a new system for applying the tax relief allowed on mortgage interest. Before this new system was introduced, the Inland Revenue worked out the amount of 'qualifying' interest you were scheduled to pay during the tax year, then this was added to your personal allowance (and any other allowance you might have had) and the whole amount was deducted from your salary before they worked out how much tax you had to pay. Although this was a viable system, in practice it involved a lot of extra work for the Revenue, particularly as mortgage interest rate changes meant fresh calculations had to be made during the year. Often first-time buyers faced a horrific first few months of their mortgage, when they had to pay out the gross amount but their payslips had not yet taken into account the extra tax relief to which they were entitled.

The Government therefore decided it would be easier (and cheaper) if the lenders did the job instead, by automatically deducting basic rate relief from the amounts they charged their borrowers. Mortgage interest relief, in other words, was to be deducted from the payments due at source – MIRAS being the convenient shorthand.

This change has not taken place without its traumas. As we shall see in Chapter 5, most building societies decided they simply could not cope with the extra work involved. They accepted the burden only on the condition that they altered the whole structure of the repayment mortgage.

Previously, the repayment mortgage involved paying a constant gross amount each month, but effectively an increasing net amount as the years went by. This came about because each payment involves two elements – interest and capital. Tax relief is available only on the interest element; in the early years, most of the payment is interest and only a little is capital repayment. Because this proportion changed every year, as the amount of capital in the monthly payments grew, it would have meant the building societies changing the 'net' payment required from borrowers every year. The majority of them refused to do so, and instead instituted the 'constant net repayment' mortgage, which, as its name implies, involves constant net payments throughout the term of the loan.

This had the advantage of reducing the administrative load of the building societies although it has not been such good news for those borrowers – typically first-time buyers – who are committing themselves to every last penny in the first years of a mortgage. The constant net repayment version is more expensive in the early years than the old-style repayment version, although over the mortgage term as a whole (usually 25 years) it works out cheaper – if you do not take inflation into account.

Higher-rate taxpayers will find they have a foot in both camps. Like everyone else, they will collect basic rate tax relief through the MIRAS system; however, relief at higher rates will continue to come through their tax codings.

From April 1987 all lenders who previously operated the MIRAS system for smaller loans are obliged to operate it for the £30,000-plus loans as well, at least as far as new borrowers are concerned. But they are under no obligation to do so for existing borrowers.

CHOOSING YOUR MORTGAGE

This chapter has contained most of the bad news home-buyers in the mid-1980s have to face. On the one hand, inflation at much lower rates means that mortgage payments are going to loom larger for much longer than before; on the other hand, house prices are increasing more slowly, making 'instant profits', except in a few exceptional areas, a thing of the past.

Then there is the fact that mortgage interest rates look set to remain uncomfortably high compared to inflation, while more and more people will face the prospect of paying part of their interest gross, without the helping hand of tax relief.

There has to be some good news, and so there is: mortgages are no longer so scarce you have to go down on your knees to beg for one, and be grateful for whatever you got. As far as mortgages are concerned, it is a buyers' market, and it is up to you to make sure you get the best possible deal.

The two main questions home-buyers are likely to ask are, how do I get a mortgage? And, how much can I borrow? Chapters 3 and 4 aim to answer these questions in as much detail as possible. But a book can only provide general answers; it is no substitute for going along to your building society or bank and asking the questions yourself.

Do not feel reluctant to do this – after all, it is their job to talk to you. There is no need to be particularly formal about it either. You may find that all you need to do is present yourself at a bank or building society's counter and say 'I want to talk to someone about mortgages' – although if you choose a particularly busy Saturday morning you might be asked to come back at some less hectic time.

Once you have established the fact that you are, in theory, eligible for a mortgage of 'xxxx' thousands of pounds, the next question to ask is – what *sort* of mortgage should I get – repayment, endowment, fixed or variable rate, or what?

In my experience, this is all too often glossed over by the

lender in a few words. Do not be rushed. Your mortgage is going to be the biggest part of your financial outgoings for a long time to come, and you can no longer rely on spiralling house prices to let you off the hook of an unwise decision made at this stage. Chapters 5 to 8 look at all the different mortgages that are available, so you can make a proper decision as to what suits you best.

CHOOSING YOUR LENDER

As well as choosing the type of mortgage you should have, you should also give some thought as to who you are going to borrow the money from. These days, the building societies do not have the field to themselves. The banks are now a major force in the mortgage market: in 1986, for example, they supplied a fifth of all the mortgage funds available – and they are not the only ones. Insurance companies are muscling into the market too. Although their share is small at the moment, it could rapidly grow.

All this competition is good for borrowers. Since the last edition of this book, just over a year ago, there have been two major changes in the mortgage scene, both of which are good news for borrowers. Firstly, size-related differentials (i.e. the more you borrow, the higher the interest rate) have practically disappeared from the scene, at least as far as the major lenders are concerned. Secondly, endowment mortgage differentials have also disappeared, once again thanks to competition.

If this is your second or third property, you will no doubt feel you have seen it all before. Size-related differentials were dropped by the societies some four years ago (due to competition from the banks) but came creeping back once the pressure was off. Who is to say the good news this time round will last? It will not necessarily but that is not the point. Once you have got your mortgage on a particular set of terms, they should stay the same for the life of the mortgage. The interest rate will change, of course, but even if endowment and size-related differentials were to reappear for new borrowers, they should not do so for those who have existing mortgages. All the more reason for borrowers to choose well now.

CHOOSING YOUR PROPERTY

All of us, naturally, hope that our property will turn out to be 'a good investment' in the future. Buyers who timed their purchase just before one of the previous property booms have been rewarded for their good timing: but it is not a factor any of us can rely on in the near future.

Another way of benefiting disproportionately from your property that has worked in the past has been to buy a run–down house in a run-down area and then to do it up while, it is hoped, the area is also 'going-up', becoming more fashionable, with prices rising to match.

This procedure follows the familiar principle of offering the prospect of greater reward for undergoing greater risk. Although quite a few areas appear to clamber up the social ladder with ease, others remain obstinately run-down (no doubt wherever we live we can all bring to mind a few examples of each).

If the area that you have chosen is not one of the lucky few, then you are unlikely to profit from such a course. Indeed, in the short term you will probably not be able to get back the money which has been spent in repairing, restoring and decorating your house when you come to sell it. And in the meantime you will have had to live in an area which, for all its potential, might have little in the way of actual attractions and plenty in the way of drawbacks.

If you want an intensive course on what sort of property and what attributes are the most valued (and therefore the most saleable) in the property market today, there is practically nothing better than to put yourself on as many estate agents' mailing lists as possible.

Of course, you will have to learn their peculiar language: 'fourth bedroom/study' usually means the 'little room at the top of the stairs which is too small even to get a bed in'; 'spacious patio' is a small backyard and – my current favourite – 'herb garden' is a patch of earth which could scarcely accommodate a bay leaf.

After you have seen a few of these properties, compare their prices and find out how quickly – or otherwise – they sell. This will give you a very accurate idea of what is a 'good buy' in property terms.

THINKING ONE STEP AHEAD

When you come to choose, it is always worth thinking one step ahead: not only, do you like it, but who else would? You may, for example, see a magnificently large – say four-bedroomed – flat which you can just afford. But who could you sell it to when you move? Families are out because, on the whole, they will be looking for somewhere with a garden. Most single people will be out because they are unlikely to be able to afford the purchase price. So are you restricting your future market for buyers to 'successful men-about-town' such as yourself? And is this wise?

What is relevant is not only the price that you will get for the property, but the speed with which you can sell it. The financial aspects matter just as much here. Not only will you find it desperately inconvenient if you have to wait for months before you receive a reasonable offer; but, if you have in the meantime found another property to move into, you will discover even a few months of a bridging loan a very expensive experience indeed.

A special mention needs to be made here of leasehold property. Most lenders are prepared to grant mortgages on leasehold properties as long as there is a reasonable length of time before the lease expires (see page 161). But before you commit yourself you should, again, think one step ahead.

If you intend to sell in, say, five years' time, will there still be ample time left for your buyer to get a mortgage as well? If the lease has 60 years to run, you should be able to get a mortgage; in five to six years' time, however, the lease could be entering the 'danger zone' where a normal 25-year mortgage may prove hard to obtain.

So, however much in your private life you may pride yourself on your magnificent eccentricity, remember when you buy your property that, like it or not, you are entering a mass market. It is a free country, and no one is going to penalise you if you have got bats in the belfry – but, if you choose to live in one, you might find you will suffer a financial punishment when you are ready to move on.

There are undeniably some disagreeable aspects to getting your first foothold on the housing ladder: for one, it costs money. In the next chapter we look at the expenses involved.

CHAPTER 2

THE COSTS OF BUYING

Whether you are buying a property for the first time, or performing the double act of buying and selling at the same time, a considerable amount of money is eaten up in the process, as you pay off all the other people who almost inevitably get involved in the transaction – estate agents (if you are selling), solicitors (unless you are determined to do it all yourself), valuers, surveyors and quite possibly, the Inland Revenue as well. When you add to this list the removal men, the cost of insurance premium for the property and extra amounts that you may have agreed to pay to the vendor for carpets, curtains and other extras, you could easily find that several thousand pounds have simply disappeared from your bank balance.

SPECIAL DEALS

Some lucky people do not have to worry, for example, employees who have to move to a different part of the country for job reasons, and whose employers have agreed to pick up the tab. Deals like this vary from company to company. Some will offer a flat sum; others will pay for everything, including the provision of an interest-free bridging loan. If your company is in the first category, make sure you read this chapter first, before you agree to anything, as it might give you second thoughts on the extent of your employer's generosity.

First-time buyers may be offered a quite different sort of special deal. In the last few years, developers have got together increasingly comprehensive 'packages' to tempt house-buyers into their arms. The perks that are offered range from free carpets and curtains, through fully-fitted kitchens complete with washing machine, tumble drier and waste disposal unit, to more abstract items such as stamp duty paid, free conveyancing, a subsidised mortgage rate for the first year and so on.

The whistle has been blown on some of these more extreme packages as some people have found to their horror that there were so many extras built in that when they came to sell, they could not attract anything like the price they originally paid.

There is no hard and fast rule as to what is a 'good' extra and what is a bad one; in any case, the picture changes over the years.

Today, for example, gas central heating is not considered an absurd luxury the cost of which you would find difficult to recoup on sale. On the contrary, it is seen as a necessity, and a flat or house without it, in some areas, could prove difficult to sell.

The moral must be, if you are offered any sort of help with moving costs, whether it comes in the shape of 'free' furniture or 'free' conveyancing, to pay special attention to the independent valuation report on the property, as this is the nearest you will get to an objective assessment of what the place is worth.

ESTATE AGENTS

If you are a first-time buyer, there is one thing to be thankful for: the services of estate agents are free to you. However many mailing lists you get yourself put on to, however much work they do for you, it will not cost you a penny. That is fair enough, as indirectly you are providing them with their income, by eventually buying a property from their lists.

You have to remember, though, that however helpful they may seem, they are not your agents, but the seller's, and they will not necessarily be looking after your best interests.

If you are selling as well as buying, you could be paying anything between 1½ per cent and 3 per cent of the sale price for the services of an estate agent. Chapter 11 goes into more detail about this and the alternatives to using an agent.

THE DEPOSIT

The biggest cost of buying – although it is not normally thought of as such – is the deposit that you will have to find for the property itself. While those who are buying the second time around normally have no problem about finding the money, as they have built up some equity in their first property, it can be tough for the first-time buyers.

As the following chapter shows, the 'normal' amount that banks and building societies are willing to lend is 80 per cent of their valuation of the property. For first-time buyers, banks and building societies will sometimes stretch their lending up to 90 or even 100 per cent – but it can depend on whether you are pre-ared to buy a post-1960 property and steer clear of converted flats. Any lending in excess of 80 per cent usually involves paying for an insurance guarantee policy (see page 36).

Lenders understandably prefer you to have some money of your own to put down: in times of mortgage shortages you could find it is essential. But it is also a sensible idea from your point of view. If you had to move much earlier than you expected, you could be in a position where you had paid very little off from your mortgage but your property had not appreciated in price sufficiently for you to be able to afford the buying and selling expenses second time around.

As soon as you have found a property you would like to buy and agreed a price with the seller, the first cash that you will generally part with is a nominal deposit (for some reason it is usually £100) paid to the estate agent concerned, as a sign that your offer is in good faith – a system simply to ensure that people do not go round making half serious offers on a number of properties. The estate agent holds the money as stakeholder, and it is returned to you if the sale does not go through. At this point you should contact your solicitor who will ask the other party to note your interest. Apart from the deposit, no money changes hands at this stage.

VALUATION AND SURVEY FEES

The next cost to confront you is the valuation fee. Lenders will insist on this, which is understandable, given that the property you choose is going to act as security for the loan which the building society or bank is making to you; and the lender will obviously be concerned that its security is good enough.

At the same time, the valuation of the property can be useful to you – if only in a negative way. If the society's valuer turns your chosen place down flat, then you should at least have serious second thoughts about buying it. Apart from this largely negative point, however, the valuation is simply what it says. Most lenders will let you see a copy of their valuation these days (if you come across one that will not, you should certainly complain, and tell them – with around 99 per cent truth – that 'everybody else does'); but as you will see, it is likely to contain a warning to the effect that 'the valuation is not a survey and it is possible that there are defects in the property which were not discovered by the valuer in the course of his limited inspection'.

A valuation is *not* a substitute for a full survey. We cover this subject in more detail in Chapter 9. The building society valuation is costed according to the price that you have offered to pay for the property. Table 3 shows typical fees, though they will vary from lender to lender. If the valuation report is so gloomy you decide not to go ahead, some societies might be prepared to refund part of the valuation fee – they are not obliged to, though you can always ask. For banks and other lenders the valuation fee may be based on the property valuation and not the purchase price.

Table 3 Valuation fees

Purchase price	Fee★
£	£
12,000	40
15,000	45
20,000	50
25,000	55
30,000	60
40,000	65
50,000	75
60,000	80
70,000	85
90,000	90
100,000	100
101,000 to 150,000	£5 extra per £10,000
Over 150,000	By arrangement

Source: *Halifax Building Society*.
★ Plus a flat £2 fee in all cases.

ARRANGEMENT FEE

Building societies do not charge an 'arrangement fee' for mortgages, but many of the banks do – either a flat charge, or sometimes on a scale charge depending on the amount borrowed. At present, Lloyds and Midland both charge a flat £100 fee, irrespective of the amount borrowed. Barclays and National Westminster, however, make no charge.

LEGAL COSTS

Unless you have decided to do your own conveyancing – see

Chapter 9 for a detailed discussion of the pros and cons – you will also be facing legal costs, though these are not payable until *after* the purchase has gone through.

Even if you decide to do your own conveyancing, you will have to pay for the lender's solicitors. This particular element of the legal fee is based on a scale (though one disgruntled solicitor recently remarked that he would be lucky if he could charge the 'scale' fees – the conveyancing business had got so competitive).

In theory, at any rate, the fees are based on the size and type of your mortgage (endowment mortgages come more expensive) and whether the solicitor is undertaking your own legal work at the same time. If he is not, it costs more.

As for your own legal costs, these are likely to be one of the bigger items of expenditure, particularly if you are a first-time buyer. You should always ask for an estimate first; competition is working wonders with the level of fees being charged. You should check that the solicitor is acceptable to your lender otherwise you may be in for extra expense using a second firm for the lender's legal work. Examples of fees are given in Table 5.

Most solicitors will give estimates these days but remember that these can change as the work progresses if unexpected problems crop up. A few firms are now prepared to give flat quotations which will not change – this can be very useful for you when you are trying to work out your budget. Buying a flat, incidentally, is likely to mean proportionately higher fees because there is usually more work to be done, such as going through the lease.

In addition to the solicitor's actual fees, he will also charge you for 'disbursements' – money that he will have to pay out on your behalf. Land Registry fees are the largest item; the other item you are likely to see is 'local authority search fees'. These refer to questions the lawyers ask of the relevant local authority – if, for example, any planning permission has been given for a motorway at the end of the garden. You are likely to find a sum of between £12 and £20 for this on the solicitor's bill.

The Land Registry charges are worked out on a scale based on the price of the property, Table 4 gives examples. Most people are buying property that has already been registered and so will be paying the higher charges shown in the second column. A few areas in the country are not yet covered by the Land Registry, but though this means you will save on Registry charges, you may lose on the solicitor's fee, as extra work will have to be done in order to establish title to the property, and you can expect to pay for this.

Table 4 Land Registry fees

Purchase price		First registration	Dealings
£		£	£
0 –	15,000	20	20
15,001 –	20,000	25	25
20,001 –	25,000	30	30
25,001 –	30,000	35	40
30,001 –	35,000	40	50
35,001 –	40,000	50	60
40,001 –	45,000	60	70
45,001 –	50,000	70	80
50,001 –	60,000	80	90
60,001 –	70,000	90	100
70,001 –	80,000	100	125
80,001 –	90,000	110	150
90,000 –	100,000	120	175
100,001 –	150,000	140	200
150,001 –	200,000	160	225
200,001 –	300,000	180	250
300,001 –	400,000	200	275
400,001 –	500,000	220	300
500,001 –	600,000	240	325
600,001 –	700,000	260	350
700,001 –	800,000	280	375
800,001 –	900,000	300	400
900,001 –	1,000,000	325	425
1,000,001 –	1,250,000	375	475
1,250,001 –	1,500,000	425	525
1,500,001 –	2,000,000	500	600
2,000,001 & over		600	700

Where the amount of the value is a figure which includes pence, the value may be rounded down to the nearest £1.

Note: Most people will pay the higher figure, shown under the 'Dealings' column. You will pay the 'First registration' charges only if your property is in an area which has come on to the Land Registry since the property last changed hands.

STAMP DUTY

The next expense is stamp duty which is charged at a flat rate of 1 per cent on all transactions above £30,000: if your property costs £35,000, therefore, you will pay £350.

Although the rate of stamp duty was halved in the 1986 budget for share purchases, house-buyers enjoyed no such luck. Frankly, I cannot see any chance of it being abolished, or even halved, though the threshold might increase in future years. The problem with stamp duty on property is that it is just the sort of tax the Revenue loves. It is lucrative, it is cheap to collect, and given that most people only move maybe three or four times in their lives, it is bearable – unlike local authority rates, for instance which are a constant thorn in the home-owner's flesh – and one quickly forgets the pain of paying it, until the next time.

FIXTURES AND FITTINGS

Unless you are buying a newly-built house or flat, it is likely that the place will contain all sorts of shelves, cupboards, kitchen units, lighting fitments, carpets and curtains. Some of these will automatically be included in the purchase price: 'immovable' fixtures such as fitted wardrobes, kitchen units, lighting switches and so on. Others, such as carpets and curtains, may sometimes be included, or the seller may demand an extra sum of money for them.

Then there are 'free-standing' items such as cookers and fridges which it may be convenient for the seller to sell to you. You will usually find that it is cheaper – as well as a good deal more convenient – to buy these from the seller than to go out searching for new or second-hand items for yourself.

There is no 'fair price' for such things as fitted carpets or second-hand fridges. If the seller has originally acquired them for nothing from his seller, he might be happy to pass them on to you for nothing; if, on the other hand, he has recently spent hundreds of pounds having new carpets fitted, you may find you will be asked a substantial sum for them.

There is obviously some room for a bit of discreet haggling here, but do not overdo it. People are funny over financial deals and it is not unknown for a seller to withdraw from a sale because the buyer refuses to pay £200 for the carpets, even though that would represent a miniscule amount of the value of the total transaction.

MORTGAGE INDEMNITY GUARANTEE

Most lenders have two levels of lending – the 'normal' one, which is usually 80 per cent of the valuation of the property and a higher one, so long as the borrower pays for an 'indemnity guarantee' issue by an insurance company, covering the lender against your defaulting. The guarantee is automatically arranged by the lender; the cost, if you are borrowing less than 100 per cent of the valuation, can sometimes be added to your mortgage, so you pay it off in monthly instalments.

Premiums vary from around £2.80 to £4 per extra £100 borrowed above the 80 per cent mark. So if, for example, you are seeking a 95 per cent loan on a £30,000 flat, you could face a premium of £135 (£4,500 at £3 per extra £100).

THE MOVE ITSELF

You must of course remember that moving all your worldly goods from one place to another is going to cost you money. The cheapest way is to do it all yourself, with cardboard boxes begged from the local off-licence, which would often make sense in the case of first-time buyers.

If you decide to have a firm of professional removers do the job for you, it is a good idea, again, to shop around. Estimates vary: you may find yourself paying anything between £200 and £400 for the contents of an average four-bedroomed house.

If there are special difficulties – your flat is on the top floor with no lift, for example, or the place fronts on to double yellow lines making parking a problem – you will pay extra.

As you move in, you should remember that you will have various other expenses to pay: such as the fitting of gas or electric cookers.

Table 5 on page 37 shows the estimated total moving costs for three properties, at prices of £30,000, £50,000 and £80,000. These costs are only for buying; if you are making your second move, you will face extra costs, mainly estate agents' and higher legal fees (see Chapter 9). The costs are only approximate, but they are reasonably representative of what you can expect.

PROPERTY INSURANCE

One of the conditions of the mortgage, generally speaking, is that your house (the lender's security) is properly insured. Most lenders will also stipulate a figure that the place must be insured for; in many cases this will be well in excess of the purchase price. It does not necessarily mean you have got a bargain, but the insurance has to cover full replacement cost of the property.

Table 5 The costs of buying

1 Buying a property for £30,000 borrowing £24,000	£
Legal fees	(300.00)
Stamp duty	NIL
Lender's legal fees	71.50
Lender's valuation fee	62.00
Structural survey	(150.00)
Land Registry fee	40.00
Local Authority search fees	15.00
Removal costs	(150.00)
Total	**788.50**

2 Buying a property for £50,000 borrowing £40,000	
Legal fees	(500.00)
Stamp duty	500.00
Lender's legal fees	76.75
Lender's valuation fee	77.00
Structural survey	(150.00)
Land Registry fee	80.00
Local Authority search fees	15.00
Removal costs	(200.00)
Total	**1,598.75**

3 Buying a property for £80,000 borrowing £64,000	
Legal fees	(800.00)
Stamp duty	800.00
Lender's legal fees	79.25
Lender's valuation fee	85.00
Structural survey	(200.00)
Land Registry fee	150.00
Local Authority search fees	15.00
Removal costs	(300.00)
Total	**2,429.25**

Notes: Figure in brackets represent variable items where costs may be reduced by shopping around for estimates first. Remember, though, that you will have to allow extra for other costs not detailed above, for example:

1   Extra payments for fixtures and fittings;
2   Premium for buildings and contents insurance;
3   Transfer (or installation) of telephone; connection of gas or electric cooker;
4   Redirection of post;
5   Extra life assurance (if repayment mortgage is chosen);
6   Mortgage guarantee policy.

The building society legal fees shown above assume the mortgage is on a repayment basis: 'scale fees' for endowment mortgages are slightly higher (see Chapter 9 for details).

If you are buying a flat, the place is probably already covered by insurance arranged through the freeholders or their agents, in which case the lender will require proof that the building is covered and that the sum is sufficient.

If you are buying a house, procedures vary among lenders. Most building societies will arrange the insurance under a 'block policy' covering all their properties. In that case, they may ask you for the premium straight away, or they may wait until the renewal premiums become due. Chapter 10 deals with the subject of insurance in more detail. Do not forget also that you are responsible for arranging insurance of the contents of your property and this again will be an expense to be faced as you move in.

THE COSTS OF PAYING YOUR MORTGAGE

Table 6 is a guide to your net monthly repayments on the mortgage assuming it is the standard length of 25 years. Shorter term mortgages come more expensive. The figures below assume that you are taking out a Constant Net Repayment Mortgage; a 'Gross Profile' mortgage will be slightly cheaper (at any rate in the early years – see Chapter 5) while a 'Low-Cost Endowment' mortgage could be slightly more expensive.

The figures also assume that firstly you are a basic-rate taxpayer and secondly, you are borrowing £30,000 or less. If you are a higher-rate taxpayer the net cost to you will be less as you will be getting extra tax relief through your tax codings.

To work out your monthly payments for a mortgage up to

£30,000, simply multiply the applicable figure (according to the interest rate you will be paying) by the number of complete thousands you are borrowing (plus the appropriate fraction if you are borrowing an odd amount). So, for example, a £20,000 mortgage at 11.25 per cent will cost you (20 x £7.95) £150 a month net of tax relief.

When you are doing your budgeting, remember that though the mortgage is likely to be the largest cost, it is not the only regular expense you will face. You will have rates, water rates, electricity and possibly gas bills to pay, probably the telephone as well. Most of these can be paid in monthly instalments if you ask, or you can open a bank budget account to help with all the ups and downs of bill paying.

Table 6 The costs of paying a building society mortgage

Net monthly payments per £1,000 borrowed over 25 years on a Constant Net Repayment Mortgage	
Interest rate (%)	Monthly payments (£)
10.00	7.35
10.25	7.47
10.50	7.59
10.75	7.71
11.00	7.83
11.25	7.95
11.50	8.08
11.75	8.20
12.00	8.32
12.25	8.45
12.50	8.57
12.75	8.70
13.00	8.83
13.25	8.96
13.50	9.08
13.75	9.21
14.00	9.34
14.25	9.47
14.50	9.60
14.75	9.73
15.00	9.86

It is a good idea to ask your sellers how much they have been paying for the heating bills and so on; your solicitor should be asking how much the rates and water rates are. If you are buying a flat, you will also face a service charge and a yearly ground rent.

Once you have moved in, you may have to be prepared for an extra large first payment to the building society. Different societies have different cut off dates for when the first monthly payment becomes due. If you complete the purchase towards the end of a calendar month, you may have nothing to pay until the end of the following month, but at that point you will be asked to make up the arrears and possibly pay the first insurance premium for the building as well. The lender will tell you what this first payment will be as soon as they have issued the cheque to your solicitor.

CHAPTER 3

THE STEP-BY-STEP GUIDE TO BUYING YOUR HOME

Buying a place of your own almost certainly means first getting a mortgage. Whether this first stage is going to be easy or not will depend partly on a matter that is quite outside your control: the degree to which the building societies and/or banks are flush with cash.

These days getting a mortgage is like rolling off a log. The lenders have, it seems, got more money than they know what to do with and many of them are now actually advertising mortgages. And it is all thanks to competition. As we remarked in Chapter 1, building societies are no longer the only players in the mortgage game. Banks and insurance companies are rapidly becoming major forces. It is all a far cry from the days – only a few years ago – when all the talk was of a 'mortgage famine' and newspapers carried articles comparing the lengths of mortgage queues at different societies.

There are all sorts of reasons for this about-turn. As far as the banks are concerned, I suspect they are all discovering that lending to British home-buyers is a much safer bet than lending to various Third World countries. And as far as building societies are concerned, the abolition of their 'cartel' means that they are just as much in the commercial world as any other industry. If they are not getting enough money in to fund their mortgage requirement, they simply increase their savings rates to attract more.

The attitude of the Government towards National Savings has also helped, as it is no longer setting a target for National Savings. In previous years, that target had to be met each year, which meant devising especially competitive products to attract large amounts of cash. The more that went into National Savings, broadly speaking, the less went into building societies and so less was available for lending on mortgages.

This 'mortgage feast' may not last forever, so you might as well enjoy it while you can and make sure you get the best possible deal on the mortgage front.

STEP-BY-STEP GUIDE

STEP ONE

The first step, as soon as you feel the moving bug beginning to bite, is to start saving, and the logical place to put your savings is with a bank or building society. As the last chapter indicated, you will need a fair amount of cash simply to complete the move, let alone provide you with a deposit for the property. If you are thinking of borrowing from your bank rather than a building society, it would be a good idea to start building up brownie points by not going into the red at the end of every month!

A few institutions run 'preferential mortgage schemes' whereby you undertake to save a set amount every month for a set period and at the end of that time they will give you a mortgage. Have a close look at what they are offering – and particularly the rate of interest they pay. If it is lower than the going rate, it is probably not worth it: if you are prepared to be a model saver, you will stand a good chance of a mortgage anyway, whatever the situation.

So where should you put your savings? There is no harm in increasing your range of options by choosing two or three places: say, one a major building society or bank, chosen on the basis that it offers a competitive mortgage deal; two, a local lender, who might be more sympathetic to you when you come to choose your property, and are hoping to buy something a bit out of the ordinary.

Whatever you do, remember that quantity as well as quality counts: they will not be too impressed by the fact that you have been a depositor with them for 20 years, if all you have managed to save is £50!

STEP TWO

If you are a first-time buyer and are able to plan ahead, it is a good idea to take advantage of the Government-backed *Homeloan Scheme*. You have to save for at least two years with one of the savings institutions taking part in the scheme – these include building societies, the banks and Girobank.

You must sign a form giving notice of your intention to save under the scheme, and at the end of the two year stint, you are in line for two benefits:

1 A cash bonus of up to £110 (depending on the amount you have saved); and,
2 An extra loan of £600 – which is usually added to the mortgage but which is interest-free for the first five years, and on which no capital repayments are due for the first five years either.

There are various conditions attached to the scheme: for example, you must have saved at least £300 one year before you apply for the benefits, while to get the full £600 loan you must have saved at least £600 yourself. Full details are available from post offices, building societies and banks.

STEP THREE

Next stage is to go along to the building society or bank as soon as you are ready to start looking seriously for a property. Ideally, by now you should have saved enough to pay your estimated moving costs plus a decent-sized deposit.

The manager will be able to give you an idea of the amount you will be able to borrow, how much it will cost, and whether they have any caveats on the type of property they are prepared to lend on. A few lenders issue you with a Mortgage Certificate, valid for three months, which states that you are entitled to a mortgage of a certain amount. The idea is that you can take the Certificate along with you on your house-hunting trips to impress the house-sellers to whom you might want to make an offer. They are partly a gimmick; with funds so freely available, a 'guarantee' of a mortgage is less valuable than it sounds. In any case, it is not an unconditional guarantee: the amount any lender is willing to make available depends not just on the level of your income, but on the valuation of the property (see Chapter 4). Still, some Certificates do have one good feature – they save a bit of time in the long drawn out process of house purchase by getting one chore out of the way before you start – the business of taking up employers' references.

STEP FOUR

Now find your house. The major source of information on properties for sale is still to be found with estate agents and you should certainly make these your first port of call. Do not forget, however, there are several other options, depending on where you live: advertisements in local and/or national newspapers, 'property shops' which are basically a sort of computer-dating service for house-buyers and sellers (see Chapter 11 for more details).

What should you be looking for as you start out on your flat or house hunting? Some books set out solemn checklists of all the things you should be thinking about: the number of bedrooms and reception rooms, the proximity to shops, transport and schools; the direction the garden faces (determining the amount of sun it gets) and so on and so forth.

The one thing I wished I had, last time I was house hunting, was a compass, to work out which way the windows actually faced, and so be able to estimate if and when the rooms got the sun.

If you are arranging a 'hit list', viewing several properties in one day, it is a good idea to take a notebook along to jot down your immediate reactions to a place along with any other information you glean about it which is not included in the agent's 'blurb'. It is all too easy, in my experience, to find after a long hard day of viewing that you have forgotten which place was which as they all get lumped together in your exhausted mind.

The only other piece of advice I would proffer in this context is to remember the estate agent's basic principle: 'Three things matter, as far as property prices are concerned. In order of importance, they are: position, position and position'!

Apart from this, there is little general advice that can be given. House hunting is such a personal business, and if your idea of bliss is a 1950s bungalow with mock tudor beams, a Georgian front door and fake Cotswold stone cladding, well, I shan't say a word!

STEP FIVE

Now comes the stage of agreeing the price with the seller – assuming you are buying a second-hand property and not a brand new one. Some people prefer to negotiate indirectly through the estate agent, or through their solicitor, or – if it is a private sale – by letter.

I have always done it face to face with the owner; if there is a bit of embarrassment at undertaking this very un-British activity of haggling, at least it is usually on both sides. The owner is likely to have a private sticking point which he or she will not go below, just as you will have a private maximum price you cannot afford to exceed, and it is usually reasonably painless – you will find out very quickly if the two of you are going to be able to reach an agreement or not.

At this stage (outside of Scotland, that is) you are merely 'making an offer' for the property: an offer which can be accepted but which will still not be binding on either party. Your offer should be confirmed in writing to the estate agent, and the words to use are 'an offer which is subject to survey and subject to contract'.

This is when you may well be asked to put down a deposit as a sign of your good faith.

STEP SIX

Now it is back to the building society or bank manager, armed with details of the property (take the estate agent's sheet with you). You will have to fill out an application form at this stage, giving full details of the property, of your income, the size of the loan you require and so on. The lender will need some proof of your income at this stage, so be prepared to produce or arrange a letter from your employer or, if self-employed, some evidence of your earnings (see Chapter 4).

You will be asked at this stage what sort of mortgage you want: repayment, endowment or pension mortgage; so read Chapters 5 to 8 first. Finally, you must inform the lender of the name and address of your solicitor at this point. Remember you may be able to cut costs here by shopping around a few firms of solicitors first.

STEP SEVEN

Valuation is the next critical point in the process. The valuation will be carried out by (or on behalf of) the lender though it is, as you might expect, the buyer who pays for it. You may have to wait some weeks for the report to come through, particularly if you are buying in a busy period.

Most lenders allow you to see the valuation report these days; they can be reasonably detailed but they are not a full structural survey. Some offer a Homebuyers Report, in effect a combined valuation plus survey which will be cheaper than commissioning your own separate survey in addition to the lender's valuation. You can reckon on say £60 for the valuation of a £30,000 property, and perhaps £130 for the combined report, while commissioning a full survey could well cost an extra £150 on top of the valuation fee. See Chapter 9 for details.

Do not be too disheartened if the valuer places a lower price on the property than you have agreed to pay: this is quite common, as valuers tend to be cautious people. If their valuation is a great deal lower, however, you should perhaps have second thoughts. You could try going back to the seller to negotiate a reduction in the price; it is also worth seeking the advice of your solicitor, particularly if you are using a local firm. They may be able to tell you whether the discrepancy between the price and valuation is typical for the area – if it is, there is probably no need to worry overmuch.

If you are intending to stay in the place for the rest of your life (or thereabouts) then there is not a lot of point in quibbling over a relatively small amount – after all, a house is a home first, an investment second. But if it is your first buy, a staging post only to better things in the not too distant future, think carefully before you go ahead.

STEP EIGHT

Assuming you have passed through the crucial valuation hoop, the building society or bank will then (and only then) make you a formal, written offer of the amount it is prepared to lend and the terms it will lend on. Now you are off down the home straight.

This can be a nail-biting time for the house-buyer. If he is human, he is probably clocking up the fees he is going to have to pay his solicitor by constantly ringing up to find how things are progressing – only to hear gnomic utterances like 'I am still waiting for the searches'.

What the solicitor will actually be doing can be broken down into three broad areas; establishing title to the property (i.e. making sure it is genuinely the seller's to sell); making sure there is nothing nasty in the woodshed like a proposed motorway cutting its way through your back garden, and finding out details about the place itself: is it insulated in the loft? What are the rates payable? When was the central heating last serviced? If you are selling as well as buying, you will be on the receiving end of these questions – the only thing to do is grit your teeth and plough through them, even though it can sometimes seem that the other side's lawyers want to know everything including what you had for breakfast this morning before they will let their client proceed with the purchase!

STEP NINE

The next stage is the major landmark: exchange of contracts. From this point on, you and your seller are committed to seeing the contract through – in England and Wales, though not in Scotland (see separate section at the end of this chapter). It is only once this stage has been reached that there is any legal commitment. You, as buyer, will be asked to put down a deposit (usually 10 per cent of the purchase price) which is passed over to the other side's solicitors: if you then break the contract, you forfeit that deposit.

If you do not have the cash for the 10 per cent deposit, your bank will normally be happy to lend it to you, on the assumption that once the contract has been completed (which generally takes place a month after exchange) the money can be repaid, either from the proceeds of your (simultaneous) sale, or from the mortgage loan which comes through on completion. 'Open-ended' bridging – where you are borrowing money from the bank for an indefinite period, perhaps because your sale has fallen through, is a different matter altogether – see Chapter 13.

STEP TEN

Completion is the final staging post of the route. Your solicitor will arrange the mortgage side of the transaction, you collect the keys and move in.

Not every transaction proceeds as smoothly as this. What can you do if you trip up at the first obstacle, that of finding sufficient finance? The first thing to find out is why: is it the property that your lender has taken exception to, or you the borrower? Or is it because there is simply not enough mortgage money to go round, and you are one of the unlucky ones?

As far as the last possibility is concerned, it is unlikely at the present time, as the building societies have decided, for the moment at least, that their job is to provide mortgages and they will raise the price rather than diminish the supply. If the 'famine' does come back, however, there are various options you have: try the bank; try any other lender you have savings with; or enlist the help of various professional advisers in your search for a mortgage.

Mortgage brokers are the obvious but not the only people who can help in this situation. Going to a mortgage broker is likely to mean taking out an endowment mortgage: if you want a repayment mortgage, you will have to pay a fee to the broker, but with an endowment he earns the commission from the life assurance company.

Fees are likely to be in the region of 2 per cent of the loan. Under the 1974 Consumer Credit Act, brokers are only entitled to charge fees when the mortgage is actually completed within a six month period. If it is not, you have the right to any deposit you might have paid, with the exception of the princely sum of £1 which the broker is entitled to keep.

Brokers may be members of either the Corporation of Mortgage Brokers or the British Insurance Brokers Association. These organisations should be able to give you the names and addresses of brokers in your area.

You can also try the *estate agent* you are buying the property through; many firms are also agents for a building society – or owned by one – and they may be able to prise money out of the society for a mortgage where you have failed. Your *solicitor* is another port of call: solicitors' firms often have close working relationships with one or several building societies, using them to deposit large sums of cash on behalf of their clients, and again may be able to unlock the door to a mortgage. The same goes for *accountants,* so if you are self-employed, for example, you may find your accountant can come up with the goods.

Finally, one possibility which few people are aware of is to get in touch with the personnel officer of their company. If your company has arranged a special savings scheme with a building society for its employees – and this is an increasingly common arrangement – you may find that the society is prepared to look favourably on an application for a mortgage from a source that has provided them with large amounts of deposits. Once you have got the mortgage, of course, there is no obligation to stay with your employer.

Assuming that mortgage funds are in reasonable supply, however, what options do you have if you are still finding it hard to get a big enough mortgage? If it is the fault of the property you have chosen – in other words, if the valuation does not come up to scratch, my advice is to think carefully whether you really want to go ahead. If you are sure you do, then a tour round the professional advisers described above may produce results. It could be that another bank or building society will be willing to lend a larger amount on the property; or you may have to take out a 'top-up' mortgage with an insurance company.

With a top-up mortgage, an insurance company lends an extra amount, in return for your taking out an endowment policy to cover the whole mortgage debt (including the portion you are borrowing from the building society).

The next chapter broadly outlines the rules that building societies and banks are operating at present, both as regards the amount they will lend as a percentage of the property's value, and based on the level of your income. Some lenders are more generous than others on the rules, though it is sometimes at the price of charging a higher interest rate.

HOUSE PURCHASE IN SCOTLAND

In Scotland, the route to house purchase is different: it tends to be quicker, and it is certainly more logical, than in the rest of the UK.

House-buying in Scotland centres round solicitors. Estate agents are a rarity and most property is advertised and bought via solicitors' property centres. They are rather like the 'property shops' which are beginning to appear in England: they provide details of properties for sale, but it is usually up to the purchaser to make arrangements to view them.

Once you have found a property you like, events can move quickly. Unlike the English fashion, once an offer has been made – and accepted – a firm contract exists. You should therefore have made arrangements with a firm of solicitors before you start house hunting, rather than leaving it until you have found the right place.

Once you have found a place you like, you should instruct your solicitor to inform the other side of your interest in the property. It is at this point that the lender should be contacted and a valuation arranged; assuming all goes well, you are then in a position to make a firm offer.

If the offer is accepted, then the normal legal processes start, of establishing title, making sure there are no hidden snags in the shape of new motorways to be built across the front lawn and so on.

CHAPTER 4

HOW MUCH CAN YOU BORROW – AND ON WHAT?

The most important, and probably the first, question that any house-buyer is going to ask is 'How much can I borrow?' The answer generally depends on two criteria. The lender will be looking firstly at your ability to repay the loan; but he will also be looking at the property that is going to act as security for the loan. The most that you will be able to borrow will be based on the *lower* of the figures arrived at through the use of these two guidelines.

It is not possible to give detailed information on the lending policy of all banks, building societies and other lenders, firstly because there are so many of them (148 building societies, for a start!) and secondly because lending policies change from time to time, according to the availability of funds.

Most building societies and banks have general guidelines at any one time as to how much they will lend, though often the individual branch managers have a certain amount of discretion to alter the rules if they see fit. Although this chapter should give you a general idea of what is happening, it is no substitute for going along to the branch at the time you want to buy and asking for yourself.

THE SIZE OF YOUR INCOME

Before you even start looking for a property, you will want to know roughly what price bracket you can afford. Lenders will offer you a multiple of your income: this can vary according to the amount they have to lend, but will almost certainly be between two and a half times to three times your annual income. At the time of writing most of the major banks are willing to lend three times your annual income, and the rest are offering two and three-quarter times income.

Obviously your ability to repay a loan of a given size depends not just on your income but on the mortgage interest rate. If rates rise, you will find that lenders are stricter on the amount they will lend, if they fall, you could find they are willing to stretch the rules that bit more. Most people do not borrow the maximum: in 1986 former owner-occupiers were borrowing an average of 1.92 times their income, and even first-time buyers (who might be expected to borrow relatively more) were only up to 2.03 times their income.

These rules are for a single person: for couples, both of whom are earning, there is often a choice. You can opt for two and a half to three times the 'principal' income, plus once times the second – or around twice the joint income. Incidentally, 'principal' does *not* automatically mean the male income, it means whoever earns the most.

Table 7 Income guidelines

Case One	
Couple earning £10,000 a year each	Maximum loan
Twice the joint income (£10,000 + £10,000 x 2) = 2.75 times principal income plus	£40,000
once times second (£10,000 x 2.75 + £10,000) =	£37,500
Case Two	
A earns £14,000; B earns £6,000	
Twice the joint income (£14,000 + £6,000 x 2) = 2.75 times principal income plus	£40,000
once times second (£14,000 x 2.75 + £6,000) =	£44,500

If both of you are earning about the same level of income, then you will be able to borrow more by opting for the 'twice joint income' criterion, while if one of you is earning a great deal more than the other, the two and a half (or whatever) plus one formula yields the highest result. The above example shows the difference it can make.

Many lenders stress that their 'guidelines' are just that – only guidelines, not inflexible rules, and that they look at each case on its merits. If you are a civil servant, for example, getting automatic salary increments year by year, you could find that the lenders are willing to stretch their rules a bit. On the other hand, if you are a salesman earning a relatively low basic amount but topped up with large (but fluctuating) amounts of commission, you could find the going a bit harder.

Some lenders have specific rules on what counts as 'income' for their purposes: some automatically exclude overtime, bonuses or commission of any sort, while others accept part of them. If you are in this position, you can help your case by presenting a clear summary of your earnings over the past year or so, with a letter from your employer stating that the overtime (or whatever) is regular and is likely to continue. It does not always work; sometimes lenders will ask for a guarantee from the employer that this situation will carry on – and employers are understandably reluctant to give it.

Remember, whatever you do, the lender is going to ask for a reference from your employer, so there is no point in lying about your income!

There are a few special schemes to help first-time buyers borrow more than the usual multiple of income: the Halifax Building Society, for example, runs a low-start mortgage allowing first-time buyers to borrow up to three and three-quarter times their income, as long as they have saved a sufficient deposit with the society first. There are several other 'low start' schemes around, which can sometimes offer higher multiples. These schemes can have their drawbacks, and you need to be very sure of what you are taking on before you go ahead.

SPECIAL CASES

(1) THE SELF-EMPLOYED

Self-employed people are a special case because of the difficulty in establishing what their 'income' is. The usual ruling is that they should produce three years' audited accounts, and the loan is based on the average income earned during that time. The problem is firstly that you may not have been self-employed for that length of time, and even if you were, the average is hardly likely to be a fair reflection of what you are earning now.

To make matters worse, it is the net profit figure which counts: and any self-employed person with a good accountant will have as low a net profit as possible. Not necessarily because he is fiddling the Inland Revenue, I hasten to add, but the self-employed can for example, claim various expenses – possibly the cost of travel to work and part of the running costs of his home – which all go to reduce his net profit. Once again, it is a question of making your case to the lender. If you can produce any letters from regular customers of yours, this will help; while you can suggest to your accountant that instead of sending copies of your accounts to the lender, he simply writes them an official letter, giving them his 'informed opinion' that you will be able to repay a loan of a certain size.

(2) JOINT PURCHASE

I suppose most 'couples' are in fact married; but as far as building societies and banks are concerned (they are very liberated these days), unmarried couples buying a property jointly are treated in exactly the same way as married ones.

There can be problems if a group of people, rather than a couple, are buying a property collectively. Most lenders will only take account of a maximum of two incomes; a few will accept up to four incomes. If you are buying in this way, it is a good idea to have a formal (preferably legal) agreement between all of you on what to do if one of the group wants to sell up his or her share. There is not a significant demand for joint mortgages on this basis and you may find it takes a bit of time to get one.

THE VALUE OF THE PROPERTY

The other criterion that lenders use to decide how much you are able to borrow is the property itself. As the property is acting as security for the loan, the lender will want to be sure it is adequate.

The normal maximum percentage that a building society or bank will lend is 80 per cent of the agreed purchase price or valuation, whichever is the lower. Lenders often restrict the percentage if the loan is an especially large one, and can sometimes be wary of lending a very high percentage on old (pre-1919, for example) property.

There is usually no problem over borrowing in excess of this, but you will have to pay the premium for an 'indemnity guarantee' – an insurance policy the lender takes out to cover itself against the possibility of your defaulting. The guarantee is arranged by the lender; the cost will probably be around £2.80 to £4 for every £100 you are borrowing in excess of the 80 per cent level. This can sometimes be added on to the total mortgage, so you are paying it off monthly: if you are already borrowing 100 per cent of the valuation, though, you will have to pay the cost of the indemnity guarantee separately.

Table 8 Valuation guideline

Purchase price or valuation (whichever lower) £	Maximum normal advance	Maximum advance with indemnity
	%	%
50,000	80	100★
100,000	75	95
150,000	75	90
250,000	70	80
Over 250,000	70	negotiable

Source: *Woolwich Building Society*.
★ In this case, the indemnity guarantee must be taken out for 25% of the total, not 20%.

Table 8 shows what the Woolwich Building Society's guidelines are at the present time. Most lenders follow similar rules.

FIRST-TIME BUYERS ONLY

If you are looking for a 100 per cent mortgage, you are likely to have the greatest chance of success if:
1 You are a first-time buyer;
2 The property does not cost too much;
3 The loan you are seeking is well within the multiples of income guidelines;
4 The property is modern and conventional or a purpose-built, rather than converted, flat;
5 The lender has overall sufficient funds. (At time of writing, some societies are pulling back from 100% mortgages as they are already fairly stretched.)

DIFFERENT TYPES OF PROPERTY

People have bought castles with a mortgage before now – so do not feel you will be limited to only the most conventional type of property. All the same, there can be problems obtaining a loan on certain sorts of property. Some lenders restrict the percentage they will lend on older places: the other most common categories where there can be special conditions are as follows.

FLATS

Purpose-built flats or maisonettes are generally no problem, with a couple of important caveats:

1 The lease must adequately provide for the maintenance of the common parts of the building.
2 The lease should have at least 25 or 30 years to run *after* you have completed the mortgage term – in other words, with a usual mortgage term of 25 years, the lease should have a life of at least 50 years when you buy. You should be wary, however, of buying a lease which just fits this ruling – it means that when you come to sell, your buyer will not have a chance of obtaining a normal mortgage on it. Chapter 13 looks at this special problem of declining leases in more detail.

Freehold flats
Except in Scotland, most building societies or banks do not lend on freehold flats. Some do, however, for example Barclays Bank, and the Scarborough Building Society.

Converted flats
The attitude of lenders to flats that have been converted from big old houses depends very much on where you live. Assuming the conversion work has been carried out to a reasonable standard, you are unlikely to encounter any problems in London, for instance, or other areas where conversions are common and quite saleable.

Flats above shops
These can be slightly more problematical. Lenders will insist that there is a separate entrance to the flat; a few societies will not consider them at all.

PROPERTIES WITH PART POSSESSION

Houses which have a sitting tenant in the basement could well present something of a problem to the buyer searching for a mortgage – though by the same token, they can also be a bargain, particularly if you are able to persuade the tenant to leave once you have bought the place. You will find it easier if the greater proportion of the house is vacant and if the tenanted part is self-contained.

Some lenders will not consider part possession properties at

Some lenders will not consider part possession properties at all; the majority will consider them but you may only be able to borrow a smaller amount than shown in the usual guidelines.

In general, very few properties of any sort are dismissed out of hand by lenders these days. 'Subject to valuation' and 'subject to saleability' are the two basic considerations – and they should be just as important to you as they are to the lender, as the time will come when you will want to sell.

If you are buying a place in a poor state of repair, or with some basic amenities missing, you could find that the lender withholds a certain percentage of the loan until you have had certain specified works completed. In these cases, they will pay on production of the builder's invoice, meaning you do not actually have to find the money yourself first.

RECENT DEVELOPMENTS

Not very long ago, building societies were accused of having no social conscience: they would only lend on the nicest property in the nicest areas. By doing this they were actually helping to create slums by cordoning off large areas (typically inner cities) from the benefits of owner-occupation. There has been a complete about-turn in thinking now: the emphasis is all on encouraging owner-occupation by every means possible, rehabilitating old property rather than knocking it down or leaving it to rot, and generally breathing new life into old decaying areas.

COUNCIL HOUSES

The Housing and Building Control Act 1984 increased the maximum discount that council tenants can enjoy if they wish to buy their own property. Tenants must have lived in the place for a minimum of two years to be eligible, at which point they qualify for a discount of 32 per cent off the valuation of the property, rising by 1 per cent for each further year of occupation up to a maximum of 60 per cent for buyers who have lived there for 30 years or more. The effect of the Housing and Planning Act 1986 is an increase in the maximum discount for council flats up to 70 per cent. The maximum on houses remains at 60 per cent.

SHARED OWNERSHIP SCHEMES

Shared ownership schemes are generally run by housing associations and the idea behind them is that they provide home ownership by easy stages for individuals who would not normally be able to buy a place of their own. The Housing Corporation in London will provide a list of the regional offices where further information can be found, or you can simply look through the Yellow Pages for housing associations.

Several building societies have set up their own housing association to carry out work on this basis, and there are some impressive rehabilitation/development projects underway. To find out more about what is happening in your area, the local housing association would be the best source of information.

CHAPTER 5

REPAYMENT MORTGAGES

A repayment mortgage is the simplest way of buying a property: it works just like any other loan whereby you pay interest on the capital outstanding, while also paying back part of the capital, so that at the end of the term, usually 25 years, you finally finish paying off the entire loan.

Assuming you are taking out the loan to buy your own home, you are eligible for tax relief on the interest payments, up to the first £30,000 that you borrow. All new borrowers from April 1987 should be making their payments net of basic rate relief, even if the loan is in excess of £30,000 (see the section on 'larger loans' later in the Chapter).

The most common type of repayment mortgage, as offered by nearly all the building societies, is called a 'Constant Net' repayment mortgage. The banks in the main organise their mortgage section differently – they, along with a few building societies, offer a 'Gross Profile' repayment mortgage. Constant net repayment mortgages are simple affairs for the borrower: they are organised in such a way that (assuming interest rates do not change) you pay a constant amount, month in and month out, for the entire mortgage term. The amount of capital that you are paying back rises each year, however, as Table 9 shows.

Gross profile mortgages are quite different: the loan is worked out on the basis that constant *gross* payments are made each year. But you do not make gross payments – you are paying them net of tax relief. The result is that the net amount you pay rises gradually over the whole term of the mortgage. Table 10 shows how this works in practice over a 25-year term at a mortgage rate of 11.25 per cent.

This might seem like a bad bargain, but the twist is that payments under a gross profile type of mortgage start off considerably lower than those under a constant net repayment mortgage. In fact, you do not start paying more until the beginning of year 12 in a 25-year mortgage term. Although the overall cost, when you tot up every single payment made over the 25 years, is more with a gross profile mortgage, you have to ask yourself which is worth more to you: cheaper payments right at the start of the mortgage, or in 12 to 25 years' time, when thanks to inflation the real value of your mortgage payments will have declined considerably.

Table 9 Amount of capital paid back each year – assuming a 25-year mortgage of £10,000 at 11.25%

Year	Gross profile £	Constant net repayment £
1	84	133
2	94	143
3	104	155
4	116	169
5	129	181
6	143	197
7	159	213
8	178	231
9	197	249
10	220	270
15	374	400
20	638	593
25	1087	879

Total cost of loan over 25 years including interest at 11.25%

24,766.70	23,847.00

Table 10 Monthly cost (each year) of a £10,000 mortgage at 11.25% over 25 years with basic rate tax relief at 27%

Year	Gross profile £	Constant net repayment £
1	75.46	79.49
2	75.66	79.49
3	75.89	79.49
4	76.16	79.49
5	76.45	79.49
6	76.78	79.49
7	77.14	79.49
8	77.54	79.49
9	77.99	79.49
10	78.49	79.49
15	81.97	79.49
20	87.90	79.49
25	98.01	79.49

This is the place to warn you that lenders do not all use the same system to decide how much interest you have to pay. Odd as it may seem, a mortgage at an apparently identical interest rate may cost more from some lenders than from others. Building societies will charge you interest on the amount you owed them at the start of their financial year, without giving you any credit for the repayments you have made during that year. The Trustee Savings Bank and National Westminster also use the building society method, but the other major banks charge you only on what you actually owe from day to day – which of course is less than you owed at the start of the year. The figures quoted in this book are based on the building society method. The interest figure for endowment mortgages should be the same for all lenders, because the sum you owe does not alter. The easiest way to check up is to note what Annual Percentage Rate (APR) the lender is quoting.

Table 11 The cost of mortgages per £1,000 per month for a 25-year term net of basic rate tax, for mortgages up to £30,000

Mortgage rate % p.a.	Constant net repayment £	Gross profile* £	Endowment (interest only)** £
10.00	7.35	6.94	6.08
10.25	7.47	7.06	6.23
10.50	7.59	7.18	6.38
10.75	7.71	7.31	6.53
11.00	7.83	7.43	6.69
11.25	7.95	7.55	6.84
11.50	8.08	7.68	6.99
11.75	8.20	7.81	7.14
12.00	8.32	7.93	7.30
12.25	8.45	8.06	7.45
12.50	8.57	8.19	7.60
12.75	8.70	8.32	7.75
13.00	8.83	8.45	7.90
13.25	8.96	8.58	8.06
13.50	9.08	8.72	8.21
13.75	9.21	8.85	8.36
14.00	9.34	8.98	8.51
14.25	9.47	9.12	8.66
14.50	9.60	9.25	8.82
14.75	9.73	9.39	8.97
15.00	9.86	9.53	9.12

* In first year only.
** The endowment premium has to be added to establish the total cost of the mortgage per month.
This table assumes basic rate tax relief at 27%.

How much difference does it actually make which sort of mortgage you choose? It varies slightly according to the level of the mortgage rate, but if you are borrowing £30,000, you could be saving around £12 a month (in the first year) by going for a mortgage on the gross profile basis. Table 11 gives details of the monthly payments for the two mortgages over a wide range of interest rates.

Apart from the overall greater cost of a gross profile type mortgage, there is one drawback which is more relevant to first-time buyers or others who are expecting to move again after a few years. Because you are paying less capital back in the early stages, you will have less cash in hand next time you make a move. After five years, for example, you will have paid back £527 out of a £10,000 mortgage at 11.25 per cent on the gross profile basis, but £781 on the constant net system.

Most lenders who operate the gross profile mortgage do not change your payments every time the mortgage interest rate changes, preferring instead to have a single change once a year, which takes into account all interest rate moves throughout the year. Even if there were none, your net payments would increase each year under the gross profile system, so the lenders are really killing two birds with one stone by making all the changes at one time.

Under the constant net system, most societies are still changing your payments every time the interest rate changes. But this is now happening so frequently – at least three times a year in recent times – that it is becoming an expensive business, and some societies are considering going over to the 'annual change' basis for all their mortgages. As far as the borrower is concerned, it will not make that much difference: at some time during any year you could be paying over the odds, at other times, under. But it will save you the bother of having to write to your bank to change your standing order amount every two or three months.

HIGHER-RATE TAXPAYERS

Whatever type of mortgage they have, and however small or large it is, higher-rate taxpayers get tax relief at their higher rates only through their tax coding. Payments can only be made net of basic rate tax relief.

If you really want to work out your effective net payments, as a higher-rate taxpayer, it is not that easy. You will need to know the amount of interest you are paying each year (and it changes each year, irrespective of whether you have a constant net or gross profile mortgage).

Let us take a constant net repayment mortgage over 25 years at 11.25 per cent. The net (of basic rate tax) payments you make each month for the whole term works out at £79.50 for £10,000 borrowed. However, as the amount of capital you pay back in each year increases – as you can see from Table 9 – so, inevitably, the amount of interest you pay each year declines. In year one, out of your total mortgage payments of £954 for the year, £821 of that is interest. So if, for example, you are a 40 per cent taxpayer, you deserve an extra 13 per cent tax relief on this figure (remembering that you are already enjoying basic rate tax relief at 27 per cent). In other words, you will pay £106.73 *less* tax in the year than you would if you did not have the mortgage. In year 25, on the other hand, nearly all your payments are capital. Just £75 of the total for the year represents interest. So the extra cash-in-hand you will enjoy amounts to just £9.75 – for the whole year!

The precise figures are, it seems to me, pretty much of academic interest – if of any interest at all! Though it might help you to make sense of your tax codings if you know that repayment mortgages for higher-rate taxpayers are always effectively 'low-start' mortgages where your overall outlay (after all tax relief) rises over the years.

LOANS OF MORE THAN £30,000

Up to now, all the figures in this chapter have assumed that the whole of the mortgage qualifies for mortgage interest rate relief – in other words, that you are borrowing £30,000 or less. These days, however, more than one in three building society borrowers take out larger loans, and if you ignore the first-time buyers, this other set represents more than 40 per cent. So it is worth looking at how the building societies and banks cope with these larger loans. At the moment, the arrangements are in a state of flux.

The situation is, that as from April 1987, all lenders will have to offer to their new borrowers MIRAS-type mortgages, however large the mortgage is. So if you borrow £40,000, for example, payments on the first £30,000 will be made net of tax relief and the balance, gross.

LARGER LOANS: HOW TO WORK OUT MONTHLY PAYMENTS

If you thought the section on mortgages and higher-rate tax relief was less than total simplicity, 'you ain't', as they say, 'seen nothing yet'. Borrowers in the old (non-MIRAS) system generally have the gross profile type of repayment mortgage, paying a constant gross amount each month and benefiting from tax relief through their codings. Their net payments will rise over the years in a similar (though not so marked) fashion as they do for gross profile mortgages of less than £30,000.

However, some lenders who offer only constant net repayment mortgages for those borrowing less than £30,000 have decided to use the same structure for their larger loans – Nationwide being an example. It is all very tedious but, thankfully, the difference between the two methods is not large enough to bother about too much. If you are borrowing £35,000, for example, the difference in monthly payments using the two methods comes out at around £5. And curiously enough, this difference declines the larger the loan is. What is slightly more annoying is that there is no way one can arrive at a net cost per £1,000, per month, if you are borrowing more than £30,000. The reason is obvious if you think about it. If you are borrowing £90,000, for example, two-thirds of your interest must be paid gross. If you are borrowing £35,000, just one-seventh of the interest is gross. So there simply cannot be an across the board figure of the cost.

Table 12, opposite, gives you the approximate figures (assuming your lender has opted for the constant net repayment system) for the monthly payments you will face, depending on the size of the loan.

THE TERM OF THE MORTGAGE

Most mortgages last for 25 years; this is a matter of custom only, and you can go for a shorter or (sometimes) longer term if you wish. A few societies will go as far as 35 or even 40 years, some others offer 30. The major requirement is that you finish paying off the mortgage before your normal retirement date.

Table 12 Building society net monthly payments, assuming a mortgage term of 25 years, a mortgage rate of 11.25%, and basic rate tax at 27%

Size of mortgage £	Net monthly payment £
35,000	283.18
40,000	331.43
45,000	380.71
50,000	430.41
55,000	480.34
60,000	530.39
70,000	630.70
80,000	731.18
90,000	831.74
100,000	932.36

The longer the mortgage is, the lower your monthly payments are, but the slower you pay back any capital. As you can see from Table 9, even with a 25-year mortgage you are paying the capital back at a snail's pace in the first few years, so unless you are really in a situation where every penny counts there is not a great deal of point in insisting on a longer period.

What about shorter term mortgages? Although few if any borrowers opt for these at the outset, some people effectively go on to a shorter term mortgage when they decide to keep their payments level although interest rates have gone down. This means higher monthly payments but a lower overall cost, as the following figures show:

Table 13

Term	Net monthly cost per £10,000 £	Total cost to end of term £
15 years	98.63	17,753.40
20 years	86.23	20,695.20
25 years	79.49	23,847.00

Note: Figures on a constant net repayment basis, assuming a mortgage rate of 11.25% and basic rate tax relief.

Taking out a shorter term mortgage is in effect a convenient method of saving money. How good a method of saving it is depends on the interest rates available for savers. In the following example, we have assumed someone is borrowing money at the basic mortgage rate of 11.25 per cent gross equal to 8.21 per cent net while he has managed to find a savings account that will pay him 8.5 per cent net on his savings. It is also assumed (for convenience) that he wraps up the arrangement after five years, because he moves house – though the same principles apply whatever time span you take.

In other words, if our borrower elected to take out the longer term mortgage, and put the amount he was saving every month into a savings account, he would end up marginally better off than if he had chosen the shorter term mortgage. All this really goes to prove is that you can believe your eyes when it comes to making this decision: if you can get 8.5 per cent net on your savings while paying 8.21 per cent net on your loan, you are winning. Building societies will always tell you what the net mortgage interest rate is (though rates are normally quoted gross) so it is a simple decision to make.

Table 14 Mortgage of £10,000 at 11.25%

Term of mortgage (years)	15	25
Net monthly payment	£98.63	£79.49
Amount available for saving		£19.14
Capital repaid at end of five years	£2,135.00	£781.00
Proceeds of savings account	NIL	£1,360.93
Total	£2,135.00	£2,141.93

PAYING OFF YOUR MORTGAGE EARLY

Exactly the same applies to the question of whether you should pay your mortgage off early, assuming you have the means to do so. When people come into a windfall of some sort, it is usually the first thing they do. In fact, surprisingly perhaps, it does not always make sense financially. As long as you are in a position to receive more on your savings than your borrowing costs, you should keep the mortgage going. For all that, the idea of getting the mortgage off your back is very appealing and illogical though it might be, I confess I would be tempted to do so if I came into a small fortune unexpectedly.

There are two exceptions to the rule of not paying off a mortgage early. The first concerns some bank and all building society mortgages that have only a few years to run, and the second concerns larger mortgages.

It has been calculated that the effective rate of interest rises to an average of around 15 per cent in the final 5 years of the mortgage and in the last year, it is even higher. This is because interest is calculated by some banks and all building societies according to the amount of capital outstanding at the beginning of the year. This is explained more fully at the beginning of this chapter. There is no way you can earn that sort of money on your savings, so you might as well pay the balance off.

It is an idea to leave a nominal sum – £10 or so – still outstanding if you can, for two reasons:

1 Your building society will continue to store your title deeds for you; and
2 If you ever need to go back to borrow further sums from them – for improvements, perhaps – you count as an 'existing borrower' and might qualify for speedier treatment if societies are going through one of their mortgage famines at the time.

The second exception concerns loans of more than £30,000. There is a strong case for paying off that part of your mortgage in excess of £30,000 early. You are paying the full interest rate on these sums, and since it is impossible to recoup that money by investing your surplus cash in a savings account – particularly if you are a higher-rate taxpayer – it would be the best use of that money.

You may argue that you would rather leave your portfolio of shares (for example) intact, and keep on with your mortgage payments. That is an investment judgement that would certainly have been a good one in the last few years, as returns from stockmarkets have well exceeded the gross mortgage rate. But such a policy involves a higher level of risk, and only you can make the decision.

As to the mechanics of making partial repayments, rules differ from lender to lender. Some, like the Halifax, Midland and Lloyds Bank, will accept any amount, at any time, and credit it to your account immediately. Others will only make the appropriate interest adjustments if you pay in a minimum amount – £100 at the Abbey National, three times your normal monthly payment at the Nationwide, £500 at the Britannia.

EXTENDING THE TERM

If you get into difficulties with keeping up the mortgage payments, perhaps because the interest rate rises, you can sometimes arrange to extend the term of the mortgage instead of increasing your payments. The facility is not automatic; you will have to ask your branch manager. In case of extreme difficulties, you can sometimes go on to an interest-only basis, but this would normally only be allowed for a limited period of time, as in general, banks and building societies do not like to see the term extended beyond your retirement age.

Remember that if you have extended the term once, and interest rates rise again, room for further manoeuvres will be very limited. If you have been through a difficult patch and do not find budgeting easy at the best of times, it would be an idea to ask your lender how much you would have to pay in future to get back on course for the original term.

INSURANCE

With a repayment mortgage it is usually up to you to arrange life assurance cover for the loan. Building societies do not always insist on your taking out such insurance, though the banks usually do. Life companies have devised a special sort of insurance policy to cover mortgages; Chapter 10 gives details of the costs and considerations involved.

FIXED-RATE MORTGAGES

Fixed-rate mortgages were popular in this country in the 1930s and 1950s, and in America, they never really went out of fashion, apart from a short period a year or two back. There are signs that fixed-rate mortgages could be starting to make some headway here again: several banks have recently offered fixed rates for terms of one to three years on a limited basis. That, however, is very different from offering a fixed rate for 25 years: will we ever see the full-blooded version?

My feeling is that they are unlikely to replace the variable rate mortgages to any great extent, and we should not wish them to. Fixed-rate mortgages are essentially a very risky operation. If rates fall below the level at which you took the mortgage out, then you could lose out badly, being locked in to an expensive loan.

It is equally risky from the lender's point of view. Suppose the lender misjudged the future trend in interest rates from the other direction, and gave you a loan at what became an exceptionally cheap rate? Then, although you would be 'winning', it would be losing – in America, several savings and loan institutions (the US equivalent of building societies) simply went bust because of this.

The lender could, in theory, get round this by offering fixed-rate investments to savers, so 'matching' its liabilities and its assets. But I think, from the borrower's point of view, the risk is not worth taking. Anyone who claims to be able to forecast the level of interest rates over the next 25 years is a fool or a charlatan – or both!

CAP AND COLLAR MORTGAGES

Another recent innovation in mortgages are 'cap and collar' (or sometimes simply 'cap') mortgages. Borrowers pay a one-off premium for a measure of interest rate certainty: for example, that their mortgage rate will not go above 11.5% or below 9% for a period of three years.

To date, it has been mainly the foreign banks which have made these offers. The major point to grasp about them is that they are limited offers, depending on the level of interest rates at the time and their perceived trend. They may turn out to be good value – or a waste of money, depending on what actually happens to interest rates.

INDEX-LINKED MORTGAGES

Yet another option available is an index-linked mortgage. At present, only two organisations – neither of them building societies – are offering these to individuals: the Building Trust and the Index Linked Mortgage & Investment Company (ILMI) (for addresses, see Appendix). The mechanics in each case are slightly different, but the basic principle is the same: the mortgage starts off at a low level, with a low interest rate but payments will rise in line with inflation. But there are drawbacks as far as first-time buyers are concerned. Firstly, you have to find quite a large deposit (the two organisations will only lend between 66 per cent and 75 per cent of the valuation), and secondly, although an effectively 'low-start' mortgage sounds a good idea, a newly married couple may be looking forward to the time when the wife stops work to have children – which means there will only be one income to support the mortgage, in which case an ever rising mortgage might not be such a good idea.

On the plus side, an index-linked mortgage could mean you would be able to buy a more expensive place than you could otherwise afford – and when you bear in mind the moving costs involved in a 'trade up' this could mean you save quite a bit of money.

CHAPTER 6

ENDOWMENT MORTGAGES

An endowment mortgage is a package of two quite separate elements. In the first place there is the loan on which you pay interest for the whole of the mortgage term. Then there is an endowment policy: as the years go by, the value of the plan grows so that at the end of the mortgage term it has grown large enough to pay back all the capital of the loan and – in theory – leave you a surplus, a tax-free cash sum for your own use.

If you die before the end of the mortgage term, the endowment policy guarantees to pay off the loan. Obviously, in the early years of the term, the value of the policy itself will not be sufficient to do so. Part of the premiums you pay, therefore, go simply to cover this risk.

There are two basic types of endowment policy, 'with-profits' and 'unit-linked'. With-profits policies can be further subdivided into 'low-cost endowments' and 'full endowments'. The 'low-cost' version is the one that (nearly) everyone takes out: it is considerably cheaper than the full with-profits version, while the estimated maturity value at the end of the mortgage term is correspondingly less. The cost of unit-linked policies compares broadly with the low-cost version.

HOW WITH-PROFITS POLICIES WORK

With-profits policies have a jargon all their own. The life company invests your money in a mixture of equities, gilts and commercial property, with a view to making a long-term profit. Every year they assess how well their funds have done, and on the basis of the results, declare a 'reversionary bonus' – expressed as a percentage rate. Once declared, this bonus cannot be taken away from policy holders (although next year's bonus could be at a lower rate) – the net result being that life companies are, on the whole, fairly cautious about the level they declare at.

The life company might well be making greater profits, however, so there is a second type of bonus called a 'terminal bonus' again declared every year, but which is given *only* to policy holders whose policies are maturing that year. The terminal bonus is a much less stable thing. Roughly speaking, it represents the profits the life company has made on its investments sents the profits the life company has made on its investments (but may not have realised) as opposed to the interest or dividends it has received, which the reversionary bonus reflects.

Until last year, the quotations for life assurance policies used to follow this pattern, with two figures for the potential policy-holder to ponder: first, the sum he could expect on maturity assuming the reversionary bonus continued at its present rate, and secondly, the extra sum he could expect assuming the terminal bonus also stayed at the same level.

The problem with this was that, no matter how many lines of small print there were warning people that terminal bonuses were not to be relied on, expectations were undoubtedly raised. Terminal bonuses are currently at an all-time high, thanks to the booming equity markets. But that can't continue for ever – and life companies are not magicians. Ultimately, the returns they produce for you must depend on the performance of underlying investments and, more generally, on the stock market.

So the terminal bonus, which merely reflects the past per-formance of investments, can be a dangerously misleading thing. There's no guarantee of that sort of growth being repeated in the future.

Life companies decided last year that it would be fairer all round if they stopped quoting this 'terminal bonus'. The rever-sionary bonus rate stays in the quotation, and there is still a second figure to mull over: but it is based on an assumed growth rate of (a maximum of) 10.75 per cent. The resulting figure is generally less than it was under the old style of quotation, but for the policyholder in fact nothing has changed. Neither figure is guaranteed; all one can say is that the new-style quotations are likely to be less misleading than the old-style ones. An example of the new type of quotation is shown in Table 17.

UNIT-LINKED POLICIES

Unit-linked policies are much simpler to describe. Instead of investing your premiums in one massive pot, unit-linked companies typically have a range of funds you can choose from, with specific investment objectives. There will be an equity fund, investing only in equities, a property fund, a gilts fund – and probably some overseas-invested funds such as an American fund. You choose, in other words, where your money is going.

Your responsibility does not stop there. Unlike with-profits companies, unit-linked companies do not maintain reserves to even out any fluctuations: if the value of the fund goes up, so does the value of your policy in proportion, and if down, then the value of your policy goes down. You are getting the investment performance 'neat' so to speak. In the good times, unit-linked policies will tend to do better than with-profits policies, because none of the profits are salted away into reserves. In the bad times, there is no safety net. In other words. it is the old story of unit-linked policies involving greater risk, but providing greater potential rewards.

HOW THE BUILDING SOCIETIES AND BANKS TREAT ENDOWMENT MORTGAGES

If you are borrowing a large sum of money for a term as long as 25 years, your lender is going to be anxious firstly that you will have enough cash at the end of that time to repay the loan and secondly, that you will indeed use that money to pay them back. The second problem is solved by lenders insisting that the policy is 'assigned' to them, meaning that in law they have first call on the proceeds of the policy leaving you with whatever is left after they have taken what is owing to them.

The first is tackled by the lender insisting that you take out a policy which has a good safety margin built in; in other words the level of premiums you pay is likely to produce a sum of money a good bit in excess of the amount needed to pay off their debt.

The safety margin they build in can differ from lender to lender; for a low cost endowment policy, they usually say 'we will assume that bonuses will be added amounting to 80 per cent of reversionary bonuses attaching to the policy at maturity, on the assumption that reversionary bonuses continue to be added at the present rate. Any other form of bonus is ignored'.

As regards unit-linked policies, the usual practice is to assume a (reasonably) conservative growth rate – typically 7.5 per cent a year – so if the fund grows at à greater rate (as, on past performance, most have) again there will be a surplus for the policy holder. Unit-linked policies when used in conjunction with a mortgage also generally have a provision requiring you to pay more premiums if the fund performance does not match up to their assumptions.

Table 15 Life companies producing the best results from a 10-year endowment policy

1982	1983	1984
Equitable	Equitable	Ecclesiastical
London Life	Ecclesiastical	Equitable
UK Provident	Scottish Widows	Standard Life
Tunbridge Wells	London Life	Norwich Union
Ecclesiastical	UK Provident	Scottish Widows
Scottish Widows	Friends' Provident	Refuge

1985	1986	1987
Scottish Amicable	Standard Life	Standard Life
Standard Life	Scottish Amicable	Scottish Widows
Norwich Union	Scottish Widows	Clerical Medical
Scottish Widows	Equitable	Friends Provident
Ecclesiastical	Clerical Medical	Norwich Union
Tunbridge Wells	RNPFN	Equitable Life
		Scottish Amicable
		RNPFN
		London Life
		Tunbridge Wells
		Equitable

Source: *Money Management.*

HOW THE PREMIUM LEVELS ARE SET

The major factor determining how big your premium is going to be is the amount of your mortgage; but remember the policy also provides you with life assurance, so your age and sex come into it as well. The older you are, the higher the premiums will be for any given size of mortgage, simply because the risk of your dying before the end of the mortgage term increases. Table 16 gives a few examples at different ages.

HOW DO YOU CHOOSE A POLICY – AND HOW DO YOU JUDGE THE QUOTATIONS?

Because the lender – building society or bank – is using your policy as security for its loan, it has the last say over which company you can use. However, you are unlikely to find your choice greatly restricted; the Halifax, for example, accepts

Table 16 Low-cost endowment mortgages: premium rates per £1,000 of loan, assuming a 25-year term

Policy holder	Monthly premium
	£
Male aged 25	1.31
Female aged 25	1.31
Couple aged 30 (male) and 27 (female)	1.39
Couple aged 40 (male) and 37 (female)	1.59

Full with-profits endowment mortgage: premium rates per £1,000 of loan, assuming a 25-year term

Policy holder	Monthly premium
Male aged 25	3.59
Female aged 25	3.59
Couple aged 30 (male) and 27 (female)	3.68
Couple aged 40 (male) and 37 (female)	3.99

Source: *London Life*.
Note: To these premiums, a policy charge of £1 per month (irrespective of the size of the policy) must be added.

policies from 90 different life assurance companies. Some lenders are not keen on unit-linked policies because of the greater risk they entail.

There is, of course, no certain way that you can pick out which policy will produce the best results in 25 years' time. All you can reasonably hope to do is pick one that in the past has shown it is capable of consistently good performance. If your mortgage broker is arranging the policy for you ask him what sort of performance his chosen company has produced – if it is not a good one ask him why he has recommended it, and if you are not satisfied with the answer think about going elsewhere. It would also be wise to ask about the reserves of the life company concerned. Last year, one such company – UK Provident – was forced to stop taking on new business and to merge with another company after its own reserves dipped dangerously low. It was not a disaster for policyholders; the situation was caught long before there was any prospect of that. But it was rather worrying. So make sure you ask your broker whether his chosen company has strong reserves.

As regards past performance, we are frequently told that it is no guide to the future. But what would you do? Pick a company that had produced disappointing results up until now instead? Of course not! If you would like to do further research on this subject there are two magazines, *Money Management* and *Planned Savings,* which carry out regular comprehensive reviews of with-profits policies. Table 15 shows those companies that have produced the best results on a 10-year endowment policy in the last few years. You will see that the same names tend to crop up again and again. It does not mean, however, that some other company, perhaps just behind the leaders now, will not prove to be the winner in a future year.

Table 17 Quotation for a low-cost with-profits endowment policy

Male age not exceeding 30;
Mortgage of £25,000 repayable at the end of 25 years;
Guaranteed minimum sum payable on death of £25,000.

The cost (ignoring mortgage interest)		The benefits	
	£		£
Monthly premium	32.20	At the end of term: at 80 per cent of reversionary bonus	
Total cost of policy over term	9,660.00	projected at current rate	25,000
		If company earns a net investment return of 10.75% per annum	37,218
		Less repayment of mortgage	25,000
		Balance	12,218

Source: *Norwich Union.*
Notes: The projected sum payable will depend on bonuses earned in the future. Bonuses once added cannot be taken away.

The first thing to confront borrowers who are thinking of taking out an endowment policy is the quotation they receive, an example of which is shown in Table 17. Its content is different depending on whether it is a unit-linked policy or a with-profits one. The unit-linked companies will produce projections at an assumed growth rate, generally 7.5 per cent. Their projected results will therefore tend to be the same on paper.

Any difference between the unit-linked quotations will stem from the differing amounts of charges imposed on the policy. The projection says nothing about the past performance the company has achieved with its various funds – but it will no doubt give you information about these.

The with-profits quotations will also follow a similar pattern these days, as the cash balance shown at the bottom of the quotation depends on an assumed overall growth rate.

But, as mentioned earlier, these figures are not guaranteed. One cannot even say they are likely. Frankly, no one knows what sort of investment return the next 25 years will produce, or what sort of inflation we will have in the meantime, which itself will affect the real value – the purchasing power – of whatever cash surplus we end up with.

This is not to say we should forget about endowment policies altogether; only we should take the quotations with a healthy pinch of salt, and not believe anybody who tells you (no matter how convincingly!) that this or that will happen during the next 25 years – none of us knows. All that can be said is that the sorts of things life companies invest in – assset-backed investments such as equities and property – have in the long run proved more rewarding, and a more certain hedge against inflation, than putting your money into a building society or bank deposit account.

JOINT LIFE OR SINGLE LIFE POLICY

Endowment policies can be written either on your own life or on the 'joint lives' of yourself and your wife or husband. In practice, some companies have had so many problems issuing joint life policies to couples who have subsequently divorced that they are reluctant to issue any more, although this will not always be the case, by any means.

WHAT ABOUT ILL HEALTH?

If you have a record of bad health, you should not leap to the conclusion that you are uninsurable. Companies may sometimes ask for a written report from your doctor, and may follow this up with a medical examination conducted by another doctor on their 'panel'. This is usually only a 20 minute affair, and is not something to be alarmed at. Life companies turn away very few people – in general less than 5 per cent of prospective policy holders – for reasons of ill health, though they can 'load' premiums.

Table 18 Moving house with an endowment policy

Years	Premium for low-cost endowment policies £	+	Mortgage interest £	=	Total monthly cost £
1–4	19.20		102.60		121.80
5–7	31.38		164.16		195,54
8–25	40.08		205.20		245.28
26–29	20.88		102.60		123.48
30–32	8.70		41.40		50.10

Source: *Norwich Union*.

Table 19 Moving house with an endowment policy

	Total mortgage £	Mortgage repaid £	Mortgage out-standing £	Projected maturity value of low-cost endowment policy £	Tax-free surplus* £
Beginning of year 1	15,000	–	–	–	–
Beginning of year 5	24,000	–	–	–	–
Beginning of year 8	30,000	–	–	–	–
End of year 25	30,000	15,000	15,000	22,331	7,331
End of year 29	15,000	9,000	6,000	13,399	4,399
End of year 32	6,000	6,000	–	8,932	2,932

* The tax-free surplus is dependent on current legislation.
Note: This assumes that bonus additions will be consistent with a net investment return of 10.75% p.a.

ENDOWMENT MORTGAGES AND MOVING

If you are buying your first property with an endowment mortgage, it is very unlikely that you will be 'seeing the mortgage out'. When you move, you will usually have two options. Either you can continue with your original endowment and take out another one for the extra amount you want to borrow, or you can extend and expand your original endowment policy.

Table 20 Moving house with an endowment policy

Years	Premium for low-cost endowment policies	+ Mortgage interest	= Total monthly cost
	£	£	£
1–4	19.20	102.60	121.80
5–7	24.56	164.16	188.72
8–32	26.16	205.20	231.36

Source: *Norwich Union*.

Table 21 Moving house with an endowment policy

	Total mortgage outstanding	Projected maturity value of low-cost endowment policy	Tax-free surplus*
	£	£	£
Beginning of year 1	15,000	–	–
Beginning of year 5	24,000	–	–
Beginning of year 8	30,000	–	–
End of year 32	30,000	48,791	18,791

* The tax-free surplus is dependent on current legislation.
Note: This assumes bonus additions consistent with a net investment return of 10.75%.

The advantage of the first route lies in the fact that you will be able to pay off a portion of your total mortgage loan early, when the first policy matures. The disadvantage is that the cost of the mortgage during the middle years will be relatively more expensive.

These methods are best explained by an example. In Tables 18 and 19 we have assumed that a man aged 24 buys his first property with a £15,000 loan. What he does is to take out a fresh endowment policy each time he makes a move: the first for £15,000, the second for £9,000 and the third for £6,000. The costs of all this, after basic rate tax relief on the mortgage, are shown in Table 18. We have assumed an interest rate of 11.25 per cent throughout the term.

Table 19 shows the position as the different endowment policies come up to maturity. Most lenders will let their borrowers take the tax-free surplus at the end of year 25 and again at the end of year 29 even though there is still a mortgage debt outstanding – they know you are still paying the premiums on another policy to produce the required amount. The only circumstances in which they might be reluctant to pass the balance on to you is if you had not been keeping up with your interest payments.

The second method is simply to extend and expand your original endowment policy. Tables 20 and 21 show the costs – and the surplus – that you would get if you went by this route.

Either method is quite acceptable; most people as a matter of interest, choose the first. What you should *not* do, once you have started off on the endowment mortgage route, is to be persuaded to surrender the policy for cash, particularly in the very early years. Surrender penalties can be very high which means you will get a poor return on your money. If, for one reason or another, you have to stop paying the premiums, make the policy 'paid up' instead. This means you pay no more premiums, but you do not collect the proceeds until the end of the original term.

Occasionally, some mortgage brokers might try to persuade you when you take out a second (or third) endowment mortgage to surrender the policies you have had until now and start afresh. Do not let them persuade you. Change your broker first, not your endowment policy!

ENDOWMENT MORTGAGES FOR WOMEN

Most married people know – or believe – that one of these days they will see a mortgage through to the bitter end. It is a fair bet that most single men will be doing the same. Single women, however, can be in a rather different situation. Most young women who decide to buy their own flat look on it as a reasonably short-term venture: in three or five years' time they may get married and move on to a joint mortgage, in due course they may give up work to have children.

So what do they do with a low-cost endowment policy they may have no further use for? There are several possibilities, but it does mean that if you are in this position you have to choose your

Table 22 Options available with low-cost endowment policy
Assuming a single women of 24 takes out a low-cost endowment mortgage of £25,000 for a term of 25 years

		£
	Monthly endowment premium	31.20
1	Surrender value after 5 years.	1,754.00
2	Policy made paid up after 5 years, but left to run to end of mortgage term. Estimated maturity value:	11,498.00
3	Policy continued at full rate for full 25 years Estimated maturity value	37,218.00
4	Policy converted after 5 years to 10-year endowment, premiums continued at a full rate for following 10 years only. Estimated maturity value:	11,146.00

Source: *Norwich Union.*
Notes: All figures assume bonus additions consistent with a net investment return of 10.75%. For comparison with the amount of capital repaid on a repayment mortgage, see Table 9 in Chapter 5.

endowment policy very carefully. Table 22 shows the options available and relevant figures from Norwich Union's home loan policy. The options can be summarised as follows:
1 You can surrender the policy. This can provide fairly poor value in the early years and it should only be seen as a last resort. Until you are at least five years into the mortgage, you may not get back as much as you would have repaid under a constant net repayment mortgage – yet you could have been

paying more for the privilege.

2 You can make it 'paid up' – that is, not contribute any more premiums, and sit back and wait for the balance of the original mortgage term, at which point you collect the (reduced) proceeds.

3 You can carry on paying the premiums on the policy, and collect the full amount (with no mortgage to pay off out of it) at the end of the 25 years.

4 You can 'convert' it into a shorter term endowment, so that it runs for 10 more years, at which point you take the tax-free surplus shown at point number 4 in Table 22.

5 You can carry on paying at a reduced premium rate (which has to be at least half the original rate) and collect the correspondingly reduced proceeds.

6 If you and your husband are moving to a larger house (with a larger mortgage) you can carry on your endowment policy, using it as part of the security for the larger loan, in the manner of Tables 18 and 19. 'Mix and match' endowment mortgages along these lines are quite common.

Should a single woman bother with an endowment mortgage? One general – or depressing – point to be made is that something like one in three marriages end in divorce these days, and though no one is suggesting we should go to American lengths of drawing up pre-marriage contracts, it can surely be no bad thing to have your own independent savings plan.

If you decide to opt for the endowment, it would be sensible to keep the arrangements as flexible as possible. That means first of all, asking about surrender values before you take the policy out; secondly, asking whether the policy offers the other options outlined above. When and if you do get married and decide some change is needed, the thing to do is write to the company, telling them what your position is and asking them to come up with the relevant figures and quotations so you can decide properly.

ENDOWMENT POLICIES: PRE MARCH 13, 1984

Before the March 1984 budget, life assurance premiums qualified for 15 per cent tax relief. Premiums were payable net of the relief, meaning that for a gross premium of £10, for instance, policy holders only paid out £8.50. This enviable state of affairs finished overnight – with one important caveat. People who had existing policies at that date were allowed to continue receiving this tax relief, but only so long as they did not 'enhance the benefits' of the policy in any way, either by extending the term or by increasing the premiums and sum assured.

This ruling had two immediate effects: firstly, you should be even more determined never, ever to surrender your policy – just think of all that unrepeatable tax relief you would be wasting – and secondly, it curtails your future freedom of action as far as increasing your mortgage goes.

In Tables 18 to 21 we showed the alternative ways open to mortgage holders who are moving a step up the property ladder. The option of extending and expanding your original endowment policy is not available to you – unless you want to lose all your tax relief, that is. You will simply have to take out another, quite separate endowment policy for the extra amount you want to borrow.

GOODBYE TO DIFFERENTIALS – WHAT DOES IT MEAN?

Most lenders have now abolished the differential, the extra half per cent interest they used to charge on 'interest-only' mortgages, backed by either an endowment or pension policy. That is obviously good news for borrowers – it makes these types of mortgage cheaper. But it also effectively gives you a bit more flexibility. Suppose, for example, you are moving up from a £30,000 mortgage to a £40,000 one. You have been happy, up to now, to pay interest on the full loan for a 25-year term because, after all, you are enjoying tax relief. But once you face the prospect of paying interest gross, things do not look quite so wonderful.

We will come back to this subject again in Chapter 8, but briefly, there is no reason why you should not, if you wish, have a 'mixed' mortgage, in other words, part endowment and part repayment. In the old days, this option suffered a big drawback in that interest for the whole lot was usually set at the endowment rate which was half a per cent higher. Now there is no difference between the two, you can mix up the two methods without penalties. You could decide, for example, to take out your £40,000 mortgage with £10,000 on a repayment basis and the balance as an endowment. And then pay back the top £10,000 at a faster rate if you wish.

Make a tax efficient move. Come to us for a pension mortgage.

Last year 4,000 people made a smart move – they got the combined help of the tax-man and the Alliance & Leicester to buy their homes on a personal pension plan mortgage. We were one of the first building societies to consider lending over 35 years (rather than the usual 25) because this makes more sense if you are linking your mortgage to the longer term benefits of the pension plan. The new legislation on pensions from 1988 means that many more people will now be able to take advantage of this tax-efficient way of buying a home. If you want

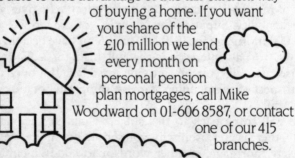

your share of the £10 million we lend every month on personal pension plan mortgages, call Mike Woodward on 01-606 8587, or contact one of our 415 branches.

ALLIANCE ✦ LEICESTER

CHAPTER 7

PENSION MORTGAGES

Linking your mortgage to a pension plan is one logical step forward from the concept of an endowment mortgage – and it is a giant leap for tax efficiency. 'Pension mortgages' were only a twinkle in a tax planner's eye at the beginning of the 1980s, but now they have become an accepted part of the mortgage scene and can offer a real alternative.

However, the 1987 budget rang a warning bell on these arrangements. A limit on the tax free cash sum available at retirement – which is used to pay off the mortgage – has been imposed for the first time. At present, it is high enough, at £150,000, not to affect any but the very rich (and well provided for in pension terms) but there is no governmental commitment to increase this figure. Should we experience another bout of high inflation, that could seem alarmingly within reach to many of us, strange as it may seem.

Certainly, in my own working lifetime of around 15 years, my salary has increased more than ten-fold – thanks far more to inflation than promotion! – and house prices, in London at any rate, by around eight times. If that sort of experience is to be repeated, that £150,000 limit could begin to seem paltry.

But for the moment, these worries are still far in the future. At present, a pension mortgage is undoubtedly the most tax efficient way of buying a house, and the limits just imposed will scarcely impede any househunter now.

WHO IS ELIGIBLE?

At least two groups are currently eligible to take out pension mortgages: the self employed and employees whose company does not provide a pension scheme; and company directors and higher paid executives, who have their own 'executive' pension plan. Different tax rules apply here and they are detailed towards the end of the chapter.

From 1988, everyone who is employed will be able to opt for a Personal Pension Plan in preference to their company's scheme: these, too, will be able to take out a pension mortgage, and we can expect to see plenty of products on the market by then.

HOW A PENSION MORTGAGE PLAN WORKS

Although a pension plan is set up mainly to provide you with an income in retirement, you are allowed to 'commute' part of the fund you have built up into a cash sum and withdraw it, free of tax, at the time you retire.

The maximum figure that can be taken as cash (subject to the overall £150,000 limit) is 25% of the total fund you have built up on retirement.

Pension plans have two great advantages over any other sort of savings vehicle. In the first place, the savings that you make qualify for tax relief – at your highest income rate, that is, between 27 per cent and 60 per cent relief (at current tax rates) on the premiums invested in a pension plan. And secondly, once your savings are inside the pension plan, they suffer neither income nor capital gains tax – again, a big advantage over ordinary endowment policies where the life company pays tax on its investments.

Pensions can therefore be seen as supremely tax-efficient savings plans which can provide you with a large cash sum on retirement. Banks and building societies have now come to realise that they can therefore provide an excellent way of paying off a mortgage.

Before lenders accepted this, however, they had to come to terms with one less fortunate aspect of pension plans: they are not assignable. In other words, you cannot give away, or sell, your rights to your pension to anyone else. The lender can therefore only hope and expect that you will pay off your mortgage with the cash sum available on your retirement: he cannot force you to do so.

Most lenders, however, have taken the view that the first charge that they have on your property is in itself a good and sufficient security. After all, this is the only security they have as regards repayment mortgages, though here, of course, capital is being repaid all the time and so the risk is not so great.

As with endowment mortgages, the interest rate differential has now been abolished on pension mortgages, and the same flat rate – currently around 11.25 per cent – applies to all types.

If you compare an endowment to a pension mortgage, two main factors stand out. The pension route is far more tax-efficient and offers better value because of this, but the figures involved are that much higher. Because of the rules on the amount that you can take as cash, compared to the amount you must take as pension, it is necessary to build up a total fund through the pension plan that is three to four times as high as the endowment result you are aiming for.

Table 23 shows an example of how this works. In the table it has been assumed that the borrower is aged 40 next birthday, a basic-rate taxpayer and taking out a mortgage of £25,000 over 25 years.

Table 23 Comparison of costs: Low–cost endowment mortgage versus pension mortgage.
For a man aged 40 next birthday, taking out a £25,000 mortgage over 25 years, basic-rate taxpayer.

Low–cost endowment		Pension	
	£		£
1 The costs			
Endowment premium	42.90	Pension premium	74.86
		+ life assurance	10.23
			85.09
		Net of 27 per cent relief	62.12
Mortgage interest	171.00	Mortgage interest	171.00
Total monthly cost	213.90	Total monthly cost	233.12
2 The proceeds			
Endowment policy	45,827.00	Pension policy	147,927.00
Less mortgage	25,000.00	Maximum cash sum	36,982.00
		Less mortgage	25,000.00
Tax-free surplus	20,827.00	Tax-free surplus plus	11,981.75
		Pension for life	14,579 p.a.

Source: *Guardian Royal Exchange.*
Note: The low-cost endowment policy illustration assumes bonuses will be added consistently with a net investment return of 10.75% p.a.

The pension policy illustration assumes bonuses will be added consistently with an investment return of 13% p.a.

As you can see from the table, the monthly premium on the pension plan, once you have added in some life assurance (which is already included in the endowment policy) comes to £85.09 compared to the endowment premium of just £42.90. However, once you take account of the tax relief available on the pension plan, the difference is whittled down to just under £20 a month.

Then take a look at the proceeds. With the endowment policies, assuming an average growth rate of 10.75 per cent over the year, there will be a tax-free surplus available for the policy holder of £20,827 – thanks to the 'safety margin' the lender will have insisted on at the beginning to determine the appropriate premium levels. The pension plan, however, produces nearly three times as much in total – thanks partly to the higher gross premiums that are going into the plan, and partly to the fact that the fund they are invested in pays no tax.

The maximum cash sum that you can take out of the fund is £36,982 which, once you have paid off the mortgage, still leaves you with a surplus of £11,981. But in addition to that, you will also have provided yourself with a pension – which at current annuity rates would be around £14,579 p.a., assuming it is to be paid throughout the lives of both your wife and yourself (a 'single life' pension, paid only until the policy holder dies, would be even higher).

If you are a higher-rate taxpayer, the pension mortgage is an even more favourable route. The pension premium for a 60 per cent taxpayer comes down to just £34.03 – already cheaper than the endowment policy, but producing over three times the benefit.

Table 24 provides another example of a pension mortgage plan, this time for a unit-linked plan, using the assumption of a 10 per cent growth rate on the plan.

THE DRAWBACKS

You should have guessed they were coming! There are limitations to this way of going about things, and you should certainly think carefully before you proceed. The following questions are the ones that you will need to ask in order to play devil's advocate with yourself before deciding.

1 WHAT ABOUT YOUR OLD AGE?

Although you are allowed to change part of your pension savings for a cash sum, you are not forced to; if you do, it will mean a lower pension than you would otherwise have had.

Are you satisfied that you still have enough to live on if you commit part of your pension savings, in advance, to paying off the mortgage?

What makes this question even more pertinent is the fact that the tax concessions on pension plans are not unlimited. If you were born in 1934 or later, you may put only 17.5 per cent of your 'net relevant earnings' (meaning, broadly, your income less trading expenses) into a pension plan. You may put in slightly more at older ages up to a maximum of 26.5 per cent but this latter figure applies only if you are 75 and still working. So do not think you can necessarily just transfer enormous sums of money into your pension plan in the last few years before you retire, to make up for any shortfall.

How serious an aspect this will be for you will depend on a number of factors: your age at the moment, how much (if any) pension provision you have made to date, and how large a mortgage you intend to have.

Table 24 Pension mortgage plan: Unit-linked version
1   Male aged 40 next birthday, retiring at 65
Mortgage of £30,000, interest rate 11.25%

Net costs per month	27% Taxpayer £	50% Taxpayer £
Mortgage interest	205.20	140.62
Pension premium	91.26	62.50
Total	296.46	203.12
Benefits at end of term	£	
1 Projected fund	188,095	
2 Maximum cash sum	47,024	
less repayment of mortgage	30,000	
3 Tax free surplus	17,024	
plus		
4 Pension for life of	18,536 p.a.	

2 Male aged 50 next birthday, retiring at 65
Mortgage of £30,000, interest rate 11.25%

Net costs per month	27% Taxpayer £	60% Taxpayer £
Mortgage interest	205.20	112.50
Pension premium	267.32	146.48
Total	472.52	258.98

Benefits at end of term	£
1 Projected fund	160,910
2 Maximum cash sum	40,227
less repayment of mortgage	30,000
3 Tax free surplus	10,227
plus	
4 Pension for life of	15,857 p.a.

Source: *Guardian Royal Exchange*.
Note: This assumes a fund growth of 13% p.a.

As a rough guide, if you have entirely neglected to put anything aside in a pension (and have no deferred pension from companies you have worked for in the past) and are much over the age of 40, then you should really be thinking of putting as much as you possibly can into your pension plan from now on, with no mortgage debts to encumber it. That is, if you want to have a reasonable pension at the end of the day.

If you are younger, you will have more leeway. But there is one trap you could fall into: that of thinking that because you have a 'pension mortgage' that means you have an adequate pension to look forward to. But look at the example in Table 23: the projected pension of £14,579 (which in itself assumes that bonuses will be added consistent with an investment return of 13% per annum) would, in real terms, be worth about £4,200 a year on the basis of a steady inflation rate of 5% a year during that time.

Under the rules, the borrower could probably put far more into his pension plan than the £74.86 a month required of him.

2 HAVE YOU NOT GOT ANYTHING BETTER TO SPEND YOUR MONEY ON?

It is quite easy, at this stage, to commit yourself to paying back money that you have not got – a long time away in the future. When you retire, however, you could well have other plans for the cash sum from the pension plan: a long holiday, home improvements, whatever. Taking out a pension mortgage means you do not have any choice – most of it will simply disappear back to the building society.

3 DO YOU WANT TO BE TOLD WHEN TO RETIRE?

It seems to be a law of nature that at 40 you are convinced you will retire at the earliest possible opportunity. At 60, however, many people think they will still carry on for a bit – and their sixty-fifth birthday finds them still hard at work, still full of plans for the future and with not a thought of retirement – particularly if they have their own business.

A pension mortgage plan is usually arranged on the basis that you will pay off your mortgage at the age of 65. It is not possible to 'part-surrender' your pension plan, that is, to take the cash part but leave the pension part for a few years more. If your plans have changed since you took the mortgage out, you may find it very inconvenient to be forced to take your pension at that particular point in time. An alternative would be to go back to your lender and ask for the mortgage to be extended for a few more years, but they may not be willing to grant this.

In fact, you can partially escape this problem if you are putting extra amounts into a pension plan, over and above the amount required for mortgage purposes. You should make sure that the extra amounts go into a separate plan – or plans – which can run for a shorter or longer time, giving you at least some flexibility and enabling you, if you wish, to 'wind down' from work over a number of years, and 'wind up' your pension at the same time.

4 ARE YOU SURE YOUR INCOME IS GOING TO BE REGULAR?

Arranging a pension mortgage plan involves committing yourself to a set level of pension premiums every year. This is all right if you are confident that your income is not going to fluctuate too much; but you might be in the sort of business where you experience massive variations in your income from year to year.

Of course, this would make life difficult for you whatever sort of mortgage you have got; but there are a couple of extra points to be borne in mind with a pension mortgage which could make it especially nasty.

Firstly, unlike mortgage interest which you pay net of the applicable rate of tax relief, pension premiums are paid gross; you receive the benefit in the shape of less tax to pay at the end of your financial year. For many self-employed people, this could mean a delay of up to 24 months. Simply in terms of cash-flow, then, this could be a problem.

Secondly, you have to remember that there are limits to the amounts that you can put into pension plans: not more than 17.5 per cent of your net relevant earnings. In most cases, this is going to be ample. But circumstances could theoretically arise where your income is not high enough to give you the allowance you need for the premiums you have to pay.

In other words, suppose you have to pay pension premiums of £150 a month in connection with your mortgage. If for any reason your net income drops below £10,290 in any one year, then you are in trouble. Your pension premium will then exceed 17.5 per cent of your earnings – although you can continue paying your premiums in, you will not get tax relief on the excess.

5 WHY SHOULD YOU PAY EXTRA COMMISSION TO THE LIFE COMPANIES?

If you were not linking your pension to a mortgage, you could save for your retirement by a series of single premium pension plans which could be adjusted each year in the light of your income earned. This is obviously more flexible, and it has another (hidden) advantage in that the rate of commission payable to intermediaries – brokers or financial advisers – is low compared to the regular premium plans, where in the first year of a plan it can be as high as 60 per cent.

6 WHAT IF YOU FALL ILL?

If you are a self-employed person and your income falls because you cannot work, you will have enough problems as it is. And even if you have covered this risk by taking out a permanent health insurance policy (to pay an income should you be ill for any extended period of time) you will be liable to face the same problems that we considered under question 4. Payments under a PHI policy do not normally count as 'earned income' and so you will not be able to qualify for tax relief on your pension plan.

An absolute necessity, if you are going to use a pension plan for your mortgage, is to choose one that incorporates a 'waiver of premium' benefit: that is, an insurance policy that will continue paying your pension premiums if you are ill.

HOW DO LENDERS TREAT PENSION MORTGAGES?

HOW MUCH WILL THEY LEND?

As with endowment policies, lenders have particular rules as to how much they will lend. Most will consider a loan that is equal to 80 per cent to 100 per cent of the anticipated cash sum available at retirement. They also make assumptions on how fast the investments in the pension fund will grow, on much the same lines as they do for endowment policies. For with-profits policies, 80 per cent of the current revisionary bonus rates are used; for unit-linked policies, an assumed growth rate of 10 per cent a year is usually made (higher than the growth rate on ordinary unit-linked endowments, reflecting the fact that the pension fund does not have to pay tax).

The other lending criteria also remain, so that getting a pension mortgage is rather like jumping a series of hurdles.
1 Is the loan for not more than 80 per cent of the valuation of the property?
2 Is it for not more than three times your income?
3 Is it for not more than 80 per cent (100 per cent) of the maximum cash sum available to you at retirement under your pension plan?
4 Is your pension plan on the 'approved list' accepted by the lender in question?

And sometimes:
5 Are you at least 35 years old?
6 Are you a 'professional person'?

Some building societies are currently restricting loans on this basis to 'professional people' in their thirties or older.

Although this might seem unfair at first sight, the point to be made (which is often obscured by the building societies themselves, in their 'mass market' approach to business) is that no one has a 'right' to a mortgage loan and the societies have to assess the credit risk in each case.

With a pension mortgage in particular, the society is granting an interest-only loan for anything up to 30 to 35 years. Although they have the 'comfort' of the fact that you are also undertaking a pension plan, they cannot have the legal security of it, as pension plans are non-assignable, so it is hardly surprising that lenders can be extremely cautious.

WHAT HAPPENS IF YOU SWITCH JOBS?

If, in mid-mortgage, you go to work for a company that runs its own pension scheme which you want to join, then you will no longer be eligible to pay premiums into a personal pension plan. So how is the mortgage to be paid off? The simplest solution is to take out a low-cost endowment policy, set to run until your retirement, so as to produce the extra sum required to pay off the mortgage. Alternatively, you could ask for your mortgage to be switched from the interest-only basis to an ordinary repayment basis.

PENSION MORTGAGES FOR DIRECTORS AND EXECUTIVES

Pension mortgage plans can also be taken out by company directors and some higher-paid executives through an 'executive pension plan'. The rules on the amounts that can be put into a pension plan (and qualify for tax relief) and the amounts that can be taken out again, at retirement as a cash sum, are different. The principle, however, remains exactly the same.

The company (and, if he wishes, the individual) may pay in sufficient premiums each year to produce a pension at retirement of up to two-thirds final salary, depending on his length of service with that company. And out of that pension, he may choose to take as a cash sum an amount equal to one and a half times his final salary – assuming, again, that he has had at least 20 years' service with that company with, again, a lower amount for a shorter period, and subject to an overall limit of £150,000.

If you are employed and belong to a company pension scheme, there is not usually any way that you can have a pension mortgage plan. However, come 1988, you will be able to opt out of your company scheme and set up your own 'portable personal pension' instead – and you will be able to effect a mortgage with one of these.

Finally it is worth remembering that if you have some freelance earnings, while still working within a company and being part of their pension scheme, you are allowed to set up a personal pension plan in respect of those freelance, 'non-pensionable' earnings. Again, that pension plan could be used for the mortgage.

If you are considering any of these 'out of the ordinary' routes to paying your mortgage, it is a good idea to seek some professional advice first.

PENSIONS AS A SOURCE OF FUNDS

Some life companies make loans available from their own resources – that is, from policy holders' funds – to borrowers who have a pension plan with that company. In times of a mortgage famine, this could be a useful extra string to your bow, though the interest rate may be slightly higher.

The loan will work in exactly the same way as a building society loan; you must not expect the requirements to be any less stringent, simply because it is the life company which is lending you the money.

Many life companies, as well as having agreements with building societies, also have special arrangements with banks which will lend money on the strength of a pension plan.

Life companies which get a request for a loan are likely to try to place it with their 'friendly' bank or building society first – and if it is turned down will see if they can accommodate it themselves. This facility can also be useful if, for example, you want money for something other than house purchase – home improvements, perhaps, or even buying a car.

PENSION AND LIFE ASSURANCE

A pension plan in itself does not contain any life assurance. Most pension plans provide for a 'return of fund' or a 'return of contributions' should you die before retirement. But it is obviously essential that you should also take out some form of life assurance to cover this risk – and most lenders (whether a building society, a bank or the life company itself) will insist on it before they lend money on this basis.

Again, the pension plan holder is favoured in this matter. If you take out a 'package deal' under your pension plan, you can benefit from full tax relief on the life assurance premiums – that is, at least 27 per cent. A maximum of 5 per cent of your 'net relevant earnings' may be devoted to life assurance – and this 5 per cent is part of, not extra to, the total allowance of 17.5 per cent allowed for pension premiums. For most people, this amount is going to be far in excess of what they are ever likely to need.

One final point needs to be made with regard to pension mortgages. If you take one out, you should always keep your options open. Suppose, for example, you took one out at the age of 40 and 15 years later you start to get worried about the level of your pension at retirement. If you are already contributing the maximum to a pension plan, now is the time to think about taking out a 10-year endowment policy to mature when you retire. You can then use the proceeds from this to pay off part or all of your mortgage, thereby giving yourself a higher pension.

CHAPTER 8

WHICH MORTGAGE TO CHOOSE?

Beggars cannot be choosers; borrowers usually can. Unless you are in a situation where mortgage money is so scarce, or your credentials for borrowing are so shaky that you are relying on a particular broker to scrape together a mortgage loan from somewhere, you will usually have a choice as to what sort of mortgage to get, and where to get it from.

The first thing to be clear about, however, is that if you really want a particular property, and it looks as if you will have to move fast in order to get it, do not hold out unnecessarily long in order to get exactly the type of mortgage you want. With a book like this, it is easy to lose sight of the wood for the trees. But, assuming the end result you are aiming for is happiness (or something along those lines), what is more important – an extra £10 or £20 a month or a place in which you are really content?

Still, the old financial gleam is bound to come back into the eye sooner or later. Assuming that you are not eligible to take out a pension mortgage as described in the last chapter, then your choice will be as follows:

Gross profile mortgage (GP)

Constant net repayment mortgage (CNR)

Low-cost endowment mortgage (LCE)

Full with-profits endowment mortgage (WP)

These four are in ascending order of cost. Assuming a mortgage interest rate of 11.25 per cent over 25 years, the cost per £1,000 per month for a basic-rate taxpayer is:

GP*	CNR*	LCE	WP
£7.55	£7.95	£8.23	£10.52

(* Calculated for a building society repayment mortgage.)

The endowment mortgage figures are only approximate. The endowment premium is based on a quotation from London Life for a couple aged 30 (male) and 27 (female). Other companies' figures may differ, but generally it is based on your age (next birthday) at the time you take out the policy. For a couple aged 40 and 37 respectively, the total net monthly cost for the low-cost endowment mortgage would be £8.43 per £1,000.

As we pointed out in Chapter 5, the cost of a gross profile

mortgage rises each year. By year 10 of a 25-year mortgage, the net monthly payment per £1,000 would have climbed to £7.85 rising to £8.20 in year 15 and £8.79 in year 20.

It is worth noting that the repayment mortgage figures do not include the cost of a mortgage protection policy, which it is sensible to take out as, unlike endowment mortgages, there is no built-in life assurance.

This all assumes that interest rates will remain at 11.25 per cent, which is extremely unlikely. At different interest rates, these relative costs alter: endowment mortgages become relatively more expensive the higher the interest rate goes and cheaper the lower it falls. For example, at a rate of 10 per cent the picture looks like this for basic-rate taxpayers.

GPCNRLCEWP
£6.94£7.35£7.47£9.68

While at 15 per cent, the position would be this:

GPCNRLCEWP
£9.53£9.86£10.52£12.81

In other words, if you have a £30,000 mortgage, at a 10 per cent basic mortgage rate you would be paying another £3.60 a month (LCE £7.47 minus CNR £7.35 = £0.12 x 30) by opting for the low-cost endowment route instead of the constant net repayment mortgage; but at 15 per cent, the gap widens to £19.80.

Whatever the interest rate, the gap between a full with-profits endowment and the other three methods is at least £70 for a £30,000 mortgage. Unless you are very rich, therefore, the full endowment is likely to be the first one you cross off the list. And even if you were that rich, there is much to be said for not putting all your savings eggs into one basket. If you can save another £70 a month, why not choose another life company – or a different form of savings, such as unit trusts?

So you are left with the first three. Many lenders do not offer a choice on the type of repayment mortgage, therefore the basic choice you have is between a constant net repayment mortgage and a low-cost endowment mortgage: a choice between jam today (in current pennies) and jam tomorrow (in possibly illusory thousands of pounds). There is simply no way of saying which is the best choice to make without having retrospective knowledge. An endowment mortgage does, however, have one characteristic that its rival lacks: an element of enforced and, in a sense, 'invisible' saving.

If you look back at the sample quotation shown in Table 17 on page 00, you can see that the total tax-free surplus could be as high as £12,218 on the basis of the assumed 10.75 per cent growth rate. Although all quotations warn you that this may not be achieved, it is not humanly possible to ignore that fact.

Suppose, instead, we were to try to adjust it for the inflation that we could suffer over the next 25 years. This is a guessing game, as much as anything else; but although we are enjoying low rates of inflation at present, remember it was only about 10 years ago that inflation was running at an annual rate of 25 per cent. That sort of level does not look in the least likely at present, but 25 years is a long time. I suspect that in the 1950s, an inflation rate of 25 per cent was simply unimaginable, which goes to show that what you can imagine may happen is not a reliable guide to what will actually happen! So let us assume a range of average inflation rates for the next 25 years. How much would that £12,218 be worth in real terms? The answers are shown below:

Average inflation rate	'Real' value of the surplus
5%	£3,604
8%	£1,784
10%	£1,124
12%	£721
15%	£366

Which one should you choose to base your decision on? I think we can knock out the highest and the lowest figures. If inflation is to continue at a steady rate of no more than 5 per cent for the next 25 years, we can expect the general level of interest rates on gilts and other fixed-interest investments to fall, the general level of property prices to remain stable and the equity market to reflect the current level of prices. These items are what the life companies invest in – and they cannot perform conjuring tricks; their bonus rates will have to be cut at some point. So you would not achieve the base figure of £12,218 in the first place. A reverse type of argument applies to the 15 per cent rate of inflation.

To cut a long story short, there is simply no way of telling whether a decision to opt for a low-cost endowment policy will turn out to be worthwhile – but then this applies to any form of long-term savings. Just do not let yourself be carried away by the apparent riches waiting for you at the end of the 25-year term!

There are two factors that may help to swing the balance in favour of endowments. The costs of the repayment mortgages shown above do not include anything for life assurance. But if you are married and certainly if you have children, this is really essential. For a man aged 30 next birthday, whose wife is a couple of years younger, such insurance will add an extra £5 a month or so to the cost of a £30,000 repayment mortgage, which just about eliminates the gap between the two. The second factor in favour of an endowment mortgage is that the policy itself can be useful in later years as another source of finance. Some (though not all) life companies are prepared to make loans to their policy holders on the security of the policy.

Finally, if you need to borrow the absolute maximum you can to finance your house purchase, you may have no alternative but to go the endowment route, as you may have to get a 'top-up' mortgage from a life company.

So far, we have looked at current cost and speculated on future returns. But there is the 'middle bit' of the mortgage to think about, too. Suppose you are buying your first property: you can expect to be there perhaps five years before you move to another place. Assuming you have taken out a mortgage of £20,000 to buy it, at the end of five years on a constant net repayment mortgage you will have paid back a total of £1,562 at a mortgage rate of 11.25 per cent.

That is the bird in the hand that a repayment mortgage provides you with. It is not a massive sum of money (and under a gross profile type of repayment mortgage it is even less – around £1,054,) but it can help; particularly when you bear in mind that the second move you make will cost proportionately more than your first as you will have the costs of selling as well as buying. Figure 2 on page 103 shows the situation in graphic form.

The second factor to consider in the 'middle portion' of the mortgage is the level of mortgage interest rates in the future. With repayment mortgages, you can in the last resort apply to extend your mortgage term if you are having trouble meeting the increased repayments. You cannot do that with an endowment mortgage, and so you would be giving up that bit of flexibility by choosing that route.

But let us look on the brighter side. Suppose that you see yourself, not as someone who is going to find it difficult to make ends meet in the future, but as one who is going to get steadily more successful and be firmly lodged in the higher-rate tax bands before you know it. In that case, the endowment route can provide you with better value for money, because the interest on the loan (up to £30,000) qualifies for full tax relief. Assuming a mortgage over 25 years at a mortgage rate of 11.25 per cent as before, and our couple taking the mortgage out are aged 30 and 27 respectively, the relative costs each month in the first year per £1,000 for higher-rate taxpayers are as follows:

Tax rate	CNR	LCE
40%	£6.73	£7.01
50%	£5.79	£6.08
60%	£4.86	£5.14

But that is not the end of the story. The constant net repayment mortgage provides constant payments throughout the term only for basic-rate taxpayers: higher-rate taxpayers pay relatively more as the term progresses, because the proportion of capital in each monthly payment rises over the years, so they get less additional tax relief. By year 10, for example, the 60 per cent taxpayer would not be paying £4.86 each month (once his extra relief is taken into account) but £5.37, a figure which will continue to rise, whereas with the endowment route, nothing changes, as his payments to the lender are 100 per cent interest throughout the term.

There has to be a warning here: higher-rate tax relief might not last indefinitely. There is something odd about the fact that the richer people are, the more help they get from the tax system to buy their own homes – and though it is extremely unlikely that basic-rate relief would ever be withdrawn (it would cause too much of an outcry!) it is not easy to be so confident about the prospects for higher-rate relief.

There is one last point to be made before we try to gather all these strands together and come up with specific recommendations. Nearly all these arguments hinge on what is going to provide the

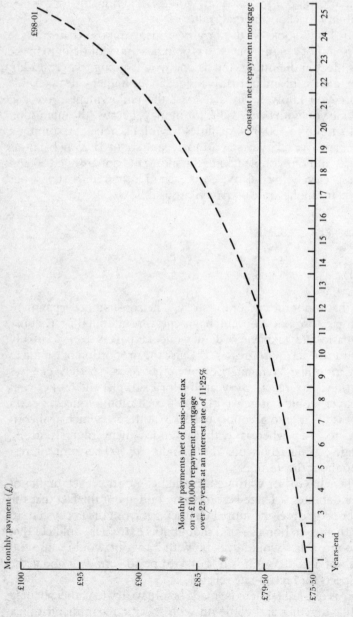

Monthly payment (£)

£100

£95

£90

£85

£79·50

£75·30

£98·01

Constant net repayment mortgage

Monthly payments net of basic-rate tax
on a £10,000 repayment mortgage
over 25 years at an interest rate of 11·25%

Years-end

1 2 3 4 5 6 7 8 9 10 11 12 13 14 15 16 17 18 19 20 21 22 23 24 25

Figure 1 Gross profile mortgage vs Constant net repayment mortgage

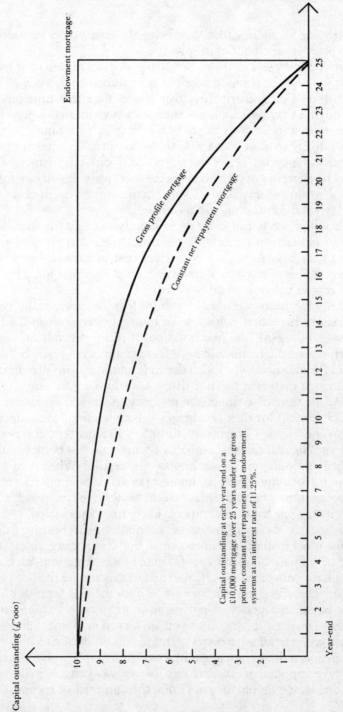

Capital outstanding (£'ooo)

Endowment mortgage

Gross profile mortgage

Constant net repayment mortgage

Capital outstanding at each year-end on a £10,000 mortgage over 25 years under the gross profile, constant net repayment and endowment systems at an interest rate of 11.25%.

Year-end

Figure 2 Capital outstanding on different types of mortgage

best value for money. But, that being the case, you cannot leave the property itself out of the picture.

If you feel you can afford to borrow an extra thousand or two by going for the cheapest possible mortgage, then it may well be worth it. This is particularly true if you are a first-time buyer (though it may well apply in other cases as well). In London and the South East for example, the very cheapest 'first-time buyer's' flat is likely to be at least £30,000. If you can afford two or three thousand pounds more, however, you can buy somewhere much better, out of proportion to the extra price. If you can, then do. It will probably hold its value better and be much easier to sell when the time comes to move.

But if property prices are rising rapidly, it could pay to go for speed rather than the best possible mortgage deal you can get. You may have to pay an extra 1 per cent in interest, but if the alternative is to stand back and watch property prices jump by 20 per cent in a year, it could be worth it.

So what mortgage should you go for? There are really two questions here: first, what *type* of mortgage? And second, who from? As regards the first question, it really depends on your own personal circumstances – a few examples are given below. And for question two, much depends on the state of play in the mortgage market at the time that you are looking for one.

At the time of writing, the majority of lenders are charging 11.25 per cent for their mortgages although a few have reduced it, mainly for new borrowers, to 10.5 to 10.8 per cent. It is fairly certain this will change, probably by the time this book is published, though one never knows for certain! When you are looking for a mortgage, the interest rate is one factor to take into account, but as far as the mainstream lenders are concerned, any advantage one has over another is likely to be short-lived.

It may be different, however, if you decide to borrow from some other institution; either a small building society, or one of the new financial institutions (in many cases American-backed) that have come into the UK mortgage market over the last year or so. These all claim that they are 'in it for the long term' and are not pursuing a policy of pulling in mortgages at a cheap rate, only to increase it later, once you are locked in. Time will tell if their protestations are correct. But if you do decide to borrow from one of these companies, make sure there are no penalties for early redemption of the mortgage. In this way you can, in the last resort, escape should they not fulfill their promise of keeping the rate competitive.

If you are shopping around for the cheapest lender, remember that the quoted interest rate tells only part of the story as far as repayment mortgages are concerned. The Annual Percentage Rate (APR) is a slightly better guide but it is still not totally satisfactory because an APR must take account of the initial setting up expenses of the loan and lenders can make different assumptions about items such as legal fees. Also, the APR does not reveal whether the lender is operating on the 'constant net' or 'gross profile' basis. Examples of the actual difference all this can make to your monthly outlay are shown in Table 25.

Table 25 Net monthly mortgage payments for a £30,000 loan over 25 years

Lender	Quoted rate	APR	Monthly outlay
Halifax	11.25	12.1	238.46
Abbey National	11.25	12.1	243.27
Nationwide	11.25	12.2	238.47
Woolwich	11.25	12.2	238.80
Lloyds	11.30	12.0	224.29
Midland	11.50	12.0	225.30
National Westminster	11.25	12.0	226.35

CHOICES

What type of mortgage should you go for? Here are some, I hope, typical examples.

A. I am a first-time buyer, unmarried, in my mid-20s, I am going to be pushed for cash whatever I do. I am buying a typical first-time buyer's flat and envisage moving in three or four years time. I am more or less at the bottom of a career ladder, but expect to do a lot better in the next few years. I do not have any dependants so do not have an immediate need for life assurance. Best choice: A gross profile repayment mortgage.

B. I am married and buying a small house. We hope to start a family while we live here. By the time we have a second child, however, we will probably have to move again to somewhere more expensive. We have not got any life assurance or savings as

yet – we think we ought to.
Best choice: A low-cost endowment mortgage.

C. I am a second – (or third) – time buyer. I am in my mid-30s with a young but growing family. We are buying a place with a larger garden and an extra bedroom – somewhere that will see us out until retirement. I do not need to borrow the maximum allowed, having done rather well on my previous property. I feel it is about time I started putting something aside for the long term.
Best choice: A low-cost endowment mortgage.

D. Like C, but I am doing well in my job and am already hit by higher-rate tax.
Choice:
1   A low-cost endowment mortgage; or
2   A full endowment mortgage.★
★ Not so advisable: start a second, separate savings plan if you can afford it.

E. I have decided to buy a place of my own, even though I am not that confident of my ability to repay. I am a salesman for a small engineering company and I would not say my job was spectacularly secure. But I would only have to pay rent otherwise – I do not have much choice.
Best choice: A repayment mortgage plus redundancy insurance, if possible.

F. I am freelance. I can count on a relatively secure income from various sources (and I expect it to be considerably higher than the 'base' figure I have done my sums on). I am in my mid-30s and have not got around to doing anything about a pension as yet.
Best choice: A pension mortgage.

Remember the Sunday newspaper that used to carry the tag line, *All human life is here*? A book on mortgages is not so different. Mortgages are only part of overall financial planning and, to consider them fully, you have to take into account all the other financial circumstances of your life: borrowing, saving, life assurance, your career, your family, your retirement.

Depending on the type of mortgage you choose, some of these aspects may already be covered within one package. But you should not neglect the rest – the aim should always be to pick out all the right pieces of the jigsaw so that you can get a complete picture whatever shape the mortgage is.

CHANGING HORSES IN MID-STREAM

What happens if you end up with the wrong sort of mortgage, or paying the wrong sort of interest rate – is there anything you can do about it?

If you realise you are paying over the odds on the interest rate side, it should be possible to 'remortgage' your property with another lender. But there are costs involved here. There could well be a fresh valuation to be paid, and there will be solicitors' fees for transferring the security from the old lender to the new one. There may also be an arrangement fee to be paid (particularly if the new lender is a bank) and – in isolated instances – an 'early redemption' charge to be paid to your old lender. The costs could mount up to £200 or more, so be clear about how much you would be saving from the move before you undertake it. If you are planning to move house shortly anyway, you might as well wait to change lenders until that time, as this will save you the extra amount. As a rough rule-of-thumb, it will take you two years to recoup a differential of a half per cent on the mortgage if you are borrowing £30,000 – assuming there are no early redemption penalties, or arrangement fees for the new loan. If you are borrowing more than this, the 'breakeven' point is considerably less, thanks to the withdrawal of tax relief at this point.

What if it is the type of mortgage that you feel is not suitable? This can be particularly important for people who have taken out pension mortgages and subsequently become ineligible to make any more contributions into the pension plan. There is normally no problem, and no charges involved, in switching between an endowment and pension mortgage, though you will have to tell the lender first and make sure that the new policy you are contemplating is acceptable to them.

It is also possible to switch from pension (or endowment) mortgage to a repayment one, though there may be a charge here (perhaps £20 or £25) for doing so. Similarly, you may also be able to switch from repayment to endowment or pension, again with a charge.

CHAPTER 9

ENLISTING THE PROFESSIONALS' HELP: CONVEYANCING AND SURVEYS

THE LEGAL SIDE

When a property is transferred from one owner to another, it is said to be conveyed, and the name for the whole process is conveyancing. What the conveyancer actually does can be summed up in a few words; if you are selling, he (or she) will prepare a contract for the sale, deal with the questions asked by the buyer's conveyancer, and ensure that the sale monies are collected and paid to you (or used to purchase your next property).

If you are buying, the conveyancer's job is to check the contract; make investigations on the property to establish among other things whether the property really is the seller's to sell; prepare the deed (known as the 'conveyance', 'transfer' or 'assignment' depending on whether the property is freehold or leasehold, and whether it is registered at the Land Registry or not) and arrange for the completion of the sale. If you are taking out a mortgage to help finance the purchase of your home, there will also be additional legal work to be carried out for the lender.

There are basically three options a house-buyer has as regards legal work at present. He can use a solicitor; he can do it himself; or he can use a non-solicitor conveyancer. In the next two to three years, we may see various other options on offer: building societies may start offering conveyancing services as part of an overall house-buying package.

SOLICITORS

The majority of house-buyers use a solicitor to carry out the conveyancing for them. There used to be 'scale fees' laid down by the Law Society for conveyancing, so there was little point in shopping around between different firms because you were likely to get the same answer. These fees were abandoned more than ten years ago, but it is only in the last two to three years the competition has really been hotting up.

Legislation is currently working its way through Parliament to abolish the solicitors' monopoly of house conveyancing – a monopoly which in fact has always been restricted – so that non-solicitor conveyancers have been able to set up in business and undertake 90 per cent of the work themselves, while there has never been anything to stop private individuals carrying out their own conveyancing.

The second big factor to influence the state of play is the relaxation of the Law Society's rules on advertising. Since 1984, firms of solicitors can advertise, and the result has been an outburst of competition which, for the moment at least, is all to the good of the consumer. Solicitors warn that cut price conveyancing is bound to lead ultimately to a decline in standards and so will, in the end, not benefit their customers at all; of course, 'they would say that' – but perhaps there is more than a grain of truth in it.

Most house purchases, however, are relatively simple affairs: up till now, consumers have been paying for (and mostly getting) an à la carte service when all they needed was something more on the supermarket level. The new relaxation could lead to some spectacular disasters; but then paying high fees to a solicitor has not always stopped spectacular disasters happening in the past.

FEES

The rule-of-thumb used to be that solicitors would charge 1 per cent of the purchase (or sale) price for conveyancing – so, if you were selling a place for £30,000 and buying one for £40,000 for example, you would face a total bill of £700 plus VAT. At the lower end of the market, particularly where the property concerned is a flat (entailing all sorts of extra work with the lease) buyers may well find they are still paying fees at this level. After all, the work involved in the conveyancing of a £20,000 flat is unlikely to be less and could even be more than the conveyancing of a £50,000 house, so there is no commercial reason why it should cost less than half as much.

It is in the upper end of the market that the biggest savings are likely to be made, and a few telephone calls could well save you a considerable amount of cash. You can obtain a list of solicitors' firms in your area by writing to the Law Society; or you can ask your building society, bank, estate agent, or local community information centres, all of whom are likely to have contacts. Finally, you can look out for advertisements in your local paper, or simply go through the Yellow Pages.

One point you should make clear if you are ringing up is whether the fees quoted are a firm price or merely an estimate, to be adjusted if the work turns out to take longer than they expected. It is becoming more common for firms to give fixed quotations.

The legal work carried out for the building society or bank which is lending you the money is a separate item which you also have to pay for. This work still has scale fees imposed by the Law Society – in theory. In practice, many solicitors do not charge the full amount. Table 26 shows what these scale fees are. The first example (1) is used where the solicitor concerned is acting for you as well as the lender; the second example (2) is where they are simply acting for the lender alone (perhaps you have decided to do your own conveyancing).

Many firms these days will 'throw in' the bank or building society work with the work they are doing for you and quote an all-inclusive figure: make sure you know exactly what basis the firm is quoting on before you go ahead. If you are using the solicitor solely for the lender's legal work, however, you could well find you are paying the full amount shown in these columns.

If you decide to use a solicitor to do your conveyancing work for you, obviously no one can say he will do an excellent job just because he (or she, of course) *is* a solicitor. But you will have safeguards. If you feel the bill is too high, you can apply to the Law Society for a 'Certificate of Remuneration'. The Society will say whether the bill is fair and reasonable; they cannot increase it but they can reduce it for you. You should not pay the bill before you complain, otherwise you lose the right.

If you are not satisfied with the Law Society's reply, you can also apply to the courts to have your bill 'taxed' and the courts may also reduce it for you. This should be done within 12 months of receiving the bill.

All solicitors have to be insured against claims for professional negligence and are covered by the Law Society compensation fund so that, for example, if your solicitor becomes bankrupt while holding your 10 per cent deposit or the full purchase amount, you will be refunded the money by the Law Society. Solicitors firms' accounts have to be submitted each year to the

Law Society for scrutiny.

Solicitors also have strict rules about keeping clients' money in a separate clients' account, and they are not allowed to work for two parties whose interests conflict.

CONVEYANCERS

The last few years has seen the emergence of non-solicitor conveyancers, who specialise solely in the business of property conveyancing.

The Administration of Justice Act 1985 provides for a new breed of "licensed conveyancers". This act has been coming into force gradually, but the first licenses should be granted in May 1987. Until now, it has been possible for non-solicitor conveyancers to undertake the process, but they have had to rely on a friendly solicitor to carry out part of the transaction.

If the conveyancer you choose is not a licensed one, you should check out the firm carefully as there have been a few cases where the buyer has lost out either through negligence or bankruptcy. If they answer no to the following questions, then be wary about going ahead as you will have no redress. Do they have, for example, professional indemnity insurance and a fidelity bonding scheme (to cover dishonesty)? Do they keep clients' money in a separate bank account?

Non-solicitor conveyancers usually charge a flat fee for their services which could well be cheaper than using a firm of solicitors, although the difference is likely to get less marked as competition increases.

THE CHOICE BETWEEN SOLICITOR AND CONVEYANCER

There is no satisfactory answer to the question 'Should I use a solicitor or a conveyancer?' There is evidence on both sides – and it is all anecdotal. In one case, yes, a conveyancer has made a mess of things. In another case, a solicitor has bungled. If you decide to use a conveyancer, remember that he will not have had to pass the Law Society examinations and that unless he is licensed, you have no protection should he turn out to be incompetent or dishonest. If you decide on a solicitor, you at least have the reassurance that he will have passed those exams and is bound by certain professional rules backed by the Law Society.

Table 26 Solicitors' fees for building society work

1 When solicitor also acts for purchase

Size of loan £	Repayment mortgage £	Endowment mortgage £
10,000	52.50	65.63
12,000	56.50	70.63
14,000	60.50	75.63
16,000	63.50	79.38
20,000	67.50	84.38
25,000	72.50	90.63
30,000	75.00	93.75
35,000	76.25	95.31
Above 35,000	Add 50p for each £5,000 (or part)	Add 62.5p for each £5,000 (or part)

2 When solicitor is acting for building society alone

Size of loan £	Repayment mortgage £	Endowment mortgage £
10,000	78.75	91.88
12,000	84.75	98.88
14,000	90.75	105.88
16,000	95.25	111.13
20,000	101.25	118.13
25,000	108.75	126.88
30,000	112.50	131.25
35,000	114.38	133.44
Above 35,000	Add 75p for each £5,000 (or part)	Add 87.5p for each £5,000 (or part)

The best reassurance, whomever you choose, is a personal recommendation from someone you know who has used them. One last point to bear in mind is that if the house purchase or sale is complicated by any other legal matter – if you are also going through a divorce, for example – then it may well be wise to have a solicitor act for you.

A few people – perhaps 1 in 100 of those who move house – choose a third option.

DOING IT YOURSELF

If you are prepared for a lot of paperwork, and believe that you have the thoroughness, perseverance and ability, there is nothing to stop you undertaking your own conveyancing yourself. There are several books on the subject to guide you through the maze – see the end of this chapter.

The most straightforward conveyancing task to undertake is that on a freehold house with a registered title. If the property is unregistered, you have to undertake a search going back 15 years in order to establish title.

Leasehold property is quite another matter. There is no such thing as a 'good standard lease' that you can look up in the local library to check whether the lease of your property is up to scratch. You may feel that you can rely on the solicitor who is acting for the building society to spot anything drastically wrong with the lease, but this could be imprudent.

The lender's solicitor will be concerned with certain aspects of the lease, but he is protecting the lender's interest, not yours; there is no reason for him to be overly concerned with clauses relating to noise, neighbours, pets or service charges which to you as the buyer could be of utmost importance.

One point that is rarely brought out in these debates about DIY versus the lawyer is the emotional aspects of house-buying. I know plenty of solicitors who will not actually do their own conveyancing but get other members of the firm to do it. Things can and do go wrong – buyers can drop out at the last minute, bridging loans may have to be organised, sellers may suddenly say they have received a higher offer – it can be a blessing therefore to have someone else coping with the administration, to negotiate with the other side's solicitor to try and put off completion if the chain is broken, and generally take the steam out of the situation.

If you decide to go ahead and undertake your own conveyancing, consider it carefully first. It is not necessarily just a matter of filling in pre-printed forms correctly but could involve a great deal of work. It would be an idea to read one of these recommended books first to get an idea of what is involved – and if you are still determined to go ahead, then good luck!

In Scotland the law on conveyancing is quite different; most of the books mentioned at the end of this chapter apply to house purchase in England and Wales. If you live in Scotland you are likely to find the DIY route a great deal harder.

SURVEYORS AND VALUERS

Very few people bother to get a full structural survey done of the property they are buying. They rely instead on the lender's valuation and if pressed would probably answer along the lines of 'if it is good enough for the bank or building society it is good enough for me', forgetting that the lender does not actually have to live in the place, and is not concerned whether you have got good value for the property, merely that it has got good security for the loan – which are two very different things!

There are two main surveyor's organisations, the Royal Institution of Chartered Surveyors and the Incorporated Society of Valuers and Auctioneers (for addresses see Appendix). Both produce leaflets on the services they offer. Alternatively, your lender can recommend a surveyor or you can look through the Yellow Pages.

These days, borrowers are allowed to see the valuation report, and though it may well cover some obvious structural points, it is not a survey and it would be unwise to rely on it.

If you are viewing a large number of properties, you might want to carry out an amateur survey of your own before you decide whether to make an offer or not. You might at least be able to form an opinion of whether the current owner could be open to offers below his asking price, while if you spot a large number of faults on your first visit, you may be able to save yourself a great deal of time and money by not going ahead with the purchase.

You will, of course, be looking at the size and layout of the rooms, the state of decoration, the garden, the neighbourhood and the general look and 'feel' of the place anyway. What you should also look out for are any outward signs that all is not well with the structure. The current owner, incidentally, is not obliged to tell you of any faults, though you can always ask.

POINTS TO WATCH

ROOFS

Take binoculars to look at the state of the chimneys and roof: are there any slates or tiles missing? Is there a good ridge line on the roof? Flat roofs can be a pain: if the drainage is not good, pools of water can collect and eventually start seeping through. This type of roof can be expensive to repair. Roofs that have 'valleys' between the houses (often found with older semi-detached or terraced houses) can also be a nuisance as all the water can collect there and the likelihood of leaks is increased.

Many first-time buyers opting for a property in the inner cities are likely to hit upon a terraced house, a maisonette or converted flat that has a slate roof. Slate was the most common roofing material used in late Victorian times when these areas were developed. If you have found such a property, the roof may well be the greatest risk area.

Slate itself is a superb material: the danger lies in the fixing nails. These may have deteriorated over the last century, making the holes in the slates bigger. Once this process begins, there is usually no satisfactory answer but to renew the whole roof. According to one surveyor, if there are minor defects visible in a slate roof, building societies are beginning to stipulate that the whole roof be completely renewed.

These points are important, as there are vast tracts of suburbs which were developed in the 1870s and 1880s and they are now beginning to get to the stage when repairs will be necessary. You might be lucky of course: the slate roof of the the first house I lived in had lasted for 130 years before it went, but once the leaks started, minor patch-up jobs had no effect and a new roof had to be installed.

THE MAIN WALLS

Look for bulges and cracks. Many houses have small settlement cracks which are not in themselves serious. Zig-zag cracks around doors and windows can be evidence of subsidence which need not be serious if they are old, but could be an indication of trouble if they are more recent. Look to see if any of the brick-work needs repointing.

DAMP

Ask if there is a damp-proof course (some old houses do not have one). Check on the state of the guttering and drainpipes, and see if there are any damp patches on the walls. Look at the condition of the door and window frames for evidence of rust, warping or rot.

INSIDE

Again, on the walls and ceilings you should look out for bulges (in walls), sagging (in ceilings), cracks or damp patches. If you can (or dare), try slipping a penknife into the woodwork of skirting boards to see if there are any signs of damp. If the wood is rotten, the knife will slip through easily and you have got problems.

Rising damp sometimes affects ground-floor rooms and can at times be seen by a 'tidemark' around the room at skirting-board level or above. Wet and dry rot affect the timbers: dry rot is worse and more expensive to correct. Woodworm is another nasty possibility. Beware if you can see a mass of small, round holes in the furniture, cupboards, understairs, etc.

Various trade associations produce leaflets that may be of use to you (see Appendix).

THE FULL SURVEY AND POSSIBLE ALTERNATIVES

Once you have found your property, it will be your decision whether to rely on a lender's valuation or arrange your own survey. Although one should not preach about the rights and wrongs – it is a free country and people should be entitled to take their own risks – it is odd that individuals, who would never dream of buying a second-hand car from someone they do not know without even opening the bonnet, seem quite happy to buy a house, costing far more money, on effectively that basis.

There is no definition of what a 'full' survey consists of, nor any scale fees laid down, however, you should ask the surveyor for a quotation. A full survey is a very detailed report which should cover every single aspect of the state of the property and its structure. It will save you money if you ask for the valuation to be carried out at the same time (this can be arranged through the bank or building society) while if for any reason you decide to commission a separate survey, either of the professional surveyors' bodies will be able to put you in touch with firms in your area.

It is occasionally possible to reduce the cost: I once had a survey done on a property I was hoping to buy, and the news was so bad, there was no point going ahead. We agreed on the phone to abandon the place, which meant there was no need for an official, typed report. The result was a few pounds knocked off the price.

There is now a convenient 'half-way' house on offer from both the Royal Institution and the Incorporated Society, called a Homebuyer's Report. This Report aims to be sufficient for the 'average house-buyer' and ought to tell him of any major structural problem that the property might have. It will not go into the details you would expect from a full structural survey, but then this might well list things you can see for yourself (for example, a cracked tile in the bathroom).

Most lenders now offer the Homebuyer's Report, though there are still a few exceptions. The cost is on a scale according to the purchase price; it may vary from lender to lender, but figures in Table 27 should be reasonably representative.

VALUATIONS AND THE MORTGAGE LOAN

The valuation plays an essential part in the process of getting a mortgage because the lenders base their percentage of lending on the valuation figure, not the price you have agreed to pay. What happens if the valuation is less than the price you have agreed on?

One thing you can be more or less certain of is that the valuation will never be *above* the agreed price! If it is within a few hundred pounds or so, there is probably no need to worry: it is common for buyers to have to pay slightly over the odds, particularly in a strongly rising property market. If the valuation is well adrift, it is time to have second thoughts. Have you agreed too high a price? Is it worth going back to the seller and trying to negotiate a reduction? Or you can try for a second opinion: first of all ask your solicitor. He is not, of course, an expert in valuations, but if he works for a local firm doing a great deal of conveyancing work in your area, he might be able to give you an off-the-cuff 'feel' of whether it is the property that is overpriced or the valuer who is overcautious. You can try approaching another lender and asking them to do a valuation – but this means paying out more money with no guarantee that it will not be a wasted effort.

If you have a large deposit to put down anyway, the financial side can be solved by opting to borrow a higher percentage (of the valuation) than you had originally bargained for. If, for example, you wanted an 80 per cent loan on a £30,000 property (i.e. you wanted to borrow £24,000) but the lender values it at

Table 27 Valuation and survey costs

Purchase price £	Valuation alone £
12,000	40
15,000	45
20,000	50
25,000	55
30,000	60
40,000	65
50,000	75
60,000	80
70,000	85
90,000	90
100,000	100
101,000 to 150,000	£5 extra per £10,000
Over 150,000	By arrangement
Plus a flat £2 fee in all cases	

Purchase price £	Homebuyer's report and valuation £
15,000	100
20,000	105
25,000	120
30,000	130
40,000	145
50,000	160
60,000	175
75,000	210
90,000	220
100,000	230
101,000 to 150,000	£10 extra per £10,000
Over 150,000	By arrangement

Source: *Halifax Building Society*.

only £29,000, you can still borrow the amount you want, but it will be 82.7 per cent of their valuation.

This may mean that you are forced to take out an indemnity guarantee for the extra amount borrowed. What I have done in such a circumstance is suggest to the seller that he knocks the cost of the guarantee off the purchase price – which seems a reasonable bargain to make.

If you want to borrow 100 per cent of the price, however, you will find things tougher. But it can be possible – see Chapter 13. Remember you could be giving hostages to fortune if you are borrowing more money than the place is actually worth.

DECISIONS, DECISIONS

If the survey reveals major problems of one sort or another, should you go ahead? You are really on your own here in making a decision. The one point I would make is that, if you are a first-time buyer, you will probably only be spending a short time in the place – two to three years maybe – before you will want to sell it again.

If you have to spend large amounts on repairs or decorations, you could lose out: you will not necessarily be able to recoup these costs in the shape of a higher selling price, immediately. Take a fitted kitchen for example. It might cost you £2,000 to install one – but if you had the house valued the next day, it may only add £1,000 to the valuation. If, on the other hand, you are contemplating buying a house which will be your home for the next 20 years then you can afford to be more relaxed. It is not important that the cost of your new fitted kitchen will not be reflected in the selling price, as it will not be for sale.

Some buyers escape all these heart searchings by opting for brand new property; others are not happy unless they are installed in an impossible-to-heat Victorian wreck, suffering one new crisis a week. Luckily there are enough of both types of buyers around to ensure that every sort of house, eventually, gets sold, even if you personally would not be seen dead in such a horrible old – or horrible new – place.

NEGLIGENCE

Occasionally, cases arise where surveyors have failed to spot a major defect, or have seriously underestimated its importance. In theory, you can then sue them for professional negligence. However, this is not as simple as it might seem. Negligence is not the same as getting it wrong: surveyors are (unfortunately) allowed to make mistakes. What has to be proved is that the surveyor did not use the level of skill and care that one would normally expect from a suitably qualified professional person. And this is always difficult to prove.

Further reading

The Conveyancing Fraud by Michael Joseph (published by himself at 27 Occupation Lane, Woolwich, London SE18)

Bradshaw's Guide to DIY House Buying, Selling and Conveyancing (Castle Books, 1 Blackdown Road, Leamington Spa CV32 6RA)

The Legal Side of Buying a House (Consumer's Association, 14 Buckingham Street, London WC2N 6DS)

Buying and Selling a House or Flat by Marjorie Giles (Pan)

CHAPTER 10

INSURANCE: YOUR HOME, YOUR CONTENTS, YOURSELF

By the time you finally set your foot on the 'Welcome' woven into the doormat you are the proud owner of an asset worth many thousands of pounds – and at the same time are deep in debt to the tune of many thousands of pounds, too.

One word should leap out from this description of your situation – 'insure': it ought to be woven into that mat. This is not an original thought – Winston Churchill started it off by proclaiming back in the 1920s 'If I had my way, I would write the word "insure" upon the door of every cottage and upon the blotting book of every public man.'

There are three main areas where insurance is important once you become a home-owner: the property itself, its contents, and you.

INSURING THE PROPERTY

A house-building insurance policy will normally cover loss or damage to the structure by disasters such as fire, explosion, storm, flood and burst pipes.

Such insurance is normally a condition of the loan, and the lender will normally need to approve the policy. In some cases the lender will choose the insurance company through whom it is arranged. You have the right, if you wish, to request another insurance company instead – which will normally be accepted by the lender as long as its terms are equally acceptable. Banks will usually leave the choice to you.

Building societies often operate a block policy system, for which premiums are charged in two ways. Either they are added to your mortgage, so that you will pay one-twelfth of the premium every month along with your mortgage payments; or you will face a lump-sum payment at the date that the building society renews its block insurance policy.

You will get a notice from the lenders saying how much the property is to be insured for: it may well be quite at variance with the purchase price. Older property, in particular, is likely to cost more to rebuild in its original state than it currently costs to buy:

as an example, an 1890 detached house was recently bought for £44,950, but the building society required it to be insured for £66,500. The insurance, of course, covers not just rebuilding: it is for 'reinstatement cost' and this includes possible demolition costs (of a useless shell) and architects' and solicitors' fees.

Since the land cannot be destroyed, the site value will remain, and, by contrast to the Victorian house mentioned above, you might find if you have bought a newly-built house in an expensive area, that the insurance cover will be for less than the price you paid.

Lenders usually insist that cover is index-linked: the index that is used is the House Rebuilding Cost Index, prepared by the Royal Institution of Chartered Surveyors (RICS). This index is recalculated each year, the RICS compile separate tables according to the age of the property and whether it is detached, a semi or terraced. Some examples are shown in Table 29.

A recent development now offered by quite a few insurance companies is a 'no limit' buildings insurance. Instead of setting an arbitrary limit on the amount paid out, these policies simply insure you for whatever it takes to rebuild the property. Apart from this, the policies are very similar to the conventional ones described above, and will cost much the same.

Just because the building society arranges the insurance, it does not mean you should not bother to read the policy to see exactly what you are covered for – and be prepared to insist on changes if you think it is not good enough. Some policies will include the cost of alternative accommodation if the house is uninhabitable due to a fire, for example, but many will not. Some cover damage to driveways and garden fences, others do not. Damage caused by subsidence is a particularly tricky one; ensure that this is not excluded, as most lenders insist on subsidence cover, and watch for a hefty excess that may be in operation, in other words, the amount that you the policy holder have to pay up first. A sum of £500 is very common here.

Reading insurance policies has a mind-numbing effect. They appear to cover so many risks that one becomes bemused by what they include, rather than noticing what is missing. You could ask your building society or solicitor what is left out, and whether there are any optional extensions you could have to cover you.

One point to remember is that though the cover will be index-linked, the 'base' sum assured will reflect the state of the property

Table 28 Cost per square foot of rebuilding

Area and type of property	Large £	Size Medium £	Small £
Pre–1920 properties			
Greater London area			
Detached	53.00	57.00	56.00
Semi-detached	51.50	52.50	52.50
Terraced	56.00	55.00	54.50
North-West and South-West			
Detached	46.50	50.00	49.00
Semi-detached	45.50	46.00	46.00
Terraced	49.00	48.00	48.00
1920–1945 properties			
Scotland and Wales			
Detached	42.00	44.00	44.00
Semi-detached	45.50	44.00	44.00
Terraced	45.50	45.00	45.00
East Anglia, East and West Midlands			
Detached	40.00	41.50	41.50
Semi-detached	43.00	41.50	41.50
Terraced	43.00	43.00	42.50
1946 to date			
Greater London area			
Detached	43.00	45.50	46.00
Semi-detached	39.00	41.50	44.50
Terraced	39.50	42.50	47.00
South-East and North-West			
Detached	37.50	40.00	40.00
Semi-detached	34.50	36.50	39.00
Terraced	34.50	37.50	41.50

Source: *Royal Institution of Chartered Surveyors (figures to September 1986).*

when the valuation was done. If you subsequently improve the place, installing a new fitted kitchen, for example, you should inform the insurers (via the building society if you have arranged the insurance through them).

Insurers have a right to cut down on your claims by the same

Table 29 Costs of building insurance: annual premiums

Area	Pre-1920 £	Type of house 1920–1945 £	1946 to date £
		Detached, medium size	
London	171	129	112
East Anglia	135	102	89
		Semi-detached, medium size	
South-East	136	93	88
Humberside	123	84	80
		Terraced, medium-size	
London	131	100	99
Scotland	108	83	83

Note: Figures are based on re-building costs as at September 1986.

proportion that you are under-insured. So if you have installed £5,000 worth of improvements to a house insured for £50,000, and omitted to tell the insurers about it, they can in theory cut down any claims you make by 10 per cent.

THE COST

The average cost of insuring a property works out at £1.75 to £1.80 per £1,000 sum insured. Based on the rebuilding costs shown in Table 28 examples of the likely premiums you will have to face are shown in Table 29.

The policy is usually taken out before you actually move into your home. The usual practice is for insurance to be arranged as soon as you exchange contracts (or make an offer in Scotland) as from that point you are committed to buying the place, even if it burns down in the meantime. Your solicitor should automatically do this for you.

Because the insurance is protecting the lender's stake in your property as well as your own, they will continue to insure it even if you fall behind with the payment of the insurance premium. In such a case, what they will do is to add the premium to your mortgage loan where it will attract interest and, if it remains unpaid, will have the effect of extending the mortgage term.

INSURING FLATS

This is usually arranged through the freeholders to cover the entire block, rather than through the building society. However, the society will want to see the policy to satisfy itself that the conditions and sum insured are acceptable. You and your solicitor should have a close look as well. There have been cases – and I was one of them – where the insurance covered the 'common parts', in other words the exterior of the building. That sounds all right, but then the lease may go on to specify exactly where the freeholder's responsibility ends, and in my case it was half way through the exterior walls. So when my living room ceiling collapsed because the roof gave up the ghost, there was no insurance to cover it.

As a leaseholder, you will normally pay your share of the insurance premiums once a year, along with the management charge. Your solicitor will usually find out in advance how much it is going to be.

INSURING THE CONTENTS

It is your responsibility to arrange insurance of the contents of your home. Although such an insurance policy covers all sorts of risks, including fire, flood, riots and falling trees, the most common cause of loss, you will not be surprised to hear, is theft.

Premium rates vary according to where you live: the most expensive are the 'high risk' (for burglary) areas such as inner London and parts of Glasgow, Manchester, Birmingham, Liverpool and other major cities. You could find yourself paying as much as £15 for every £1,000 sum insured in these areas, going down to around £4 per £1,000 in low risk rural areas.

House insurance is a competitive business these days, and it is definitely worth shopping around, either by yourself or via an insurance broker, for the best rates. In high risk areas, though, it is going to be an expensive business whoever you choose, and your contents insurance could well cost more than the insurance of the building. But as the Building Societies Association's leaflet on the subject points out, 'It is easy for a burglar to steal valuable contents . . . but not nearly as easy for him to steal the house itself'.

SAFEGUARDS

The Association of British Insurers provides a free leaflet called *Beat the Burglar* (for address, see Appendix). It suggests certain safeguards that everyone should take: the type of locks and bolts to be used, window locks, door chains and so on. If you ask at your local police station, they will come along and advise you on the necessary safeguards and preventions.

Most opinion is against locking interior doors; once the burglars are inside your house, they will simply smash the doors down, just giving you more damage and mess to clear up.

Burglar alarms can be a good idea as long as they are properly installed; a few insurance companies reduce their premiums in consideration of this, but the majority do not do so. Unless the installation has been done correctly, the risk is not lessened. The cost of going to check installations has put off insurance companies from granting a discount. Anyway, there are certain areas (particularly in London) where you are unlikely to get insurance at all unless you already have a burglar alarm.

It is a good idea to keep a description of the valuable property you possess together with serial numbers. A lot of stolen property which is recovered by the police can never be returned to their owners because it cannot be positively identified by them. For the same reason, if you have unusual prints, paintings or jewellery, for example, you could take a photograph of the objects in question – it will all help.

You can also buy marker pens which you use to write your post code on to items such as the television, video recorder, etc. The lettering is invisible except under ultra–violet light.

Some insurance companies are beginning to offer discounts – typically between 5 per cent and 15 per cent – on their premiums if you have a burglar alarm system installed by a firm approved by them. A full alarm system is likely to cost between £400 and £1,200 to install, so it will be some time before you recoup that cost in terms of reduced insurance premiums! I do wonder whether such a system is worth it, for the average house. Not because the systems might not be efficacious, but because they can only work if they are switched on! And according to the latest statistics, two-thirds of all burglaries take place in empty houses where a window has been left open.

THE SUM INSURED

The ABI has another leaflet, also free, called *A Guide to Home*

Contents Insurance which includes a checklist of all the items you are likely to possess. The idea is that you complete the list with approximate values to arrive at the total amount for which you should insure. It really is worth going through this process, because you will be surprised at how much the sum will come to.

In my own case, five minutes' thought led me to the conclusion that I needed double the sum insured that I had first thought of – and I do not suppose this is at all untypical. Most policies require separate details of expensive articles over a certain limit and will usually expect no individual item to be worth more than 5 per cent of the total sum insured.

WHAT THE POLICIES COVER

Most policies, as mentioned above, will provide cover for your home contents being lost or damaged through fire, theft, escape of water from tanks or pipes, oil leaking from fixed heating systems, storm and flood, riot or malicious acts, explosion and lightning, impact by aircraft, vehicles or animals, falling trees, subsidence or earthquakes. They may also include accidental damage to mirrors and glass tops in furniture. This cover only applies while the contents are in the home; if you have an item you frequently use outside the home, like a camera, you will have to arrange extra cover for this. Other insurance that you can 'add on' to the basic contents insurance includes deep freezer insurance and caravan or boat insurance.

THE BASIS OF COVER

There are two alternatives: you can choose either 'indemnity' cover or 'replacement as new'.

A policy on the indemnity basis will pay you basically for the second-hand value of your possessions that have been burnt, stolen, etc. A 'replacement as new' policy will provide you with enough cash to go out and buy new items to replace the lost ones (though this does not normally apply to clothes or to household linen, where you have to be satisfied with the indemnity basis).

Many insurance companies also have an index-linked clause so that your sum insured automatically rises each year in line with the Retail Price Index.

All insurance policies require you to insure all your contents for their 'full value' (which will differ according to whether you have opted for the 'second-hand' or 'new' basis). It is important that you do: in some cases, if it becomes apparent that you have under-insured, the insurance company will reduce your claim payments by the same proportion, even if you are not claiming as much as the whole of your sum insured.

Policies covering replacement value are obviously going to be more expensive than second-hand value ones. In my opinion, however, the former are the only sort worth taking out – and they should be index-linked. If you have accepted the need for insurance, then it is totally illogical to insure for only, say, half the cost of a new television set or carpet.

COMBINED POLICIES

Some building societies are offering combined buildings and contents insurance in one package. The advantage with these policies is that if you have a global disaster of some sort – say, your pipes burst – there is no squabble over which policy covers what. The disadvantage is that these policies tend to over–insure on the contents side, as the general rule is that you are insured for an identical amount on each side, so that if your flat cost £30,000, your contents will also be insured for £30,000.

If you do have separate policies and need to make a claim on both, the general ruling is that if an item is fixed, it comes under the building policy (thus including, for example, kitchen cabinets) while if it is moveable, it is contents. Fitted carpets, however, do not follow this rule as they usually come under contents insurance.

MORE INFORMATION

The Association of British Insurers has a third free leaflet: *Buildings Insurance for Home Owners*.

INSURING YOURSELF

The third and possibly the most important item that should be insured in connection with your house purchase is you. If you have chosen an endowment mortgage, you will automatically be insured to the extent that if you die the mortgage will be paid off – though whether this is sufficient insurance or not is a different matter, as the next section shows.

If you have chosen a repayment mortgage, however, it will be up to you to arrange a policy. Mortgage Protection Policies (MPPs for short) are tailor-made for this situation. The sum that you are insured for under this type of policy decreases over the 25-year term, as you are slowly paying off the capital from the mortgage. At any point in time, in theory, the amount the policy will pay up matches the amount you have outstanding on the mortgage.

Table 30 shows some typical rates for this type of policy, assuming a mortgage rate of 14 per cent. If the interest rate goes up, premium rates could also go up, as you may be paying the loan off more slowly. And remember that if, for any reason, you stop paying your mortgage, or ask for the term to be extended because you cannot afford the payments, you must inform the insurance company. Otherwise, if you died, the proceeds of the policy might not be sufficient to cover the outstanding loan.

Table 30 Cost of mortgage protection policy (assuming interest rate of 14 per cent)

Sex	Age next birthday	Mortgage amount £	Mortgage term (years)	Monthly premium £
M	25	20,000	25	1.63
M	25	25,000	25	1.92
M	25	30,000	25	2.20
M/F	30/28	25,000	25	4.00
M/F	35/33	25,000	25	6.00
M/F	40/38	25,000	25	9.92
M/F	45/43	30,000	20	15.20

Source: *Equitable Life*.

If you do die during the mortgage term, who gets the money? It depends on what sort of mortgage you have. If you have an endowment mortgage, the proceeds automatically go to the lender, as the policy is assigned to them. The lender then takes what is due to him, and the surplus (if any) is passed on to your heirs.

With a repayment mortgage, the situation is different. Building societies do not insist that you take out one of these policies; if you do, it is your own business and the policy does not have to be assigned to them. This means that the proceeds can be paid straight to your heirs, who then have a choice whether to use it to wipe out the debt or keep the money and continue to pay the mortgage. This could be a sensible move where both parties are high earners.

If your mortgage is with a bank, however, you will find they generally insist on your taking out insurance, and want the policy assigned to them, in which case they get the proceeds.

THE NEED FOR LIFE ASSURANCE – AND THE OPTIONS

There is only one circumstance, I think, where it may not be necessary to take out life assurance in connection with your mortgage – if you are single with no dependants, but with near-relations who you are confident could cope with the matter of selling-up your property and redeeming the loan.

Remember, though, it can take some months to complete a sale. If you take out a very high percentage mortgage and die shortly afterwards, it is possible that, because of the selling expenses and the accruing interest on your unpaid mortgage, your heirs might actually face a large net loss on the whole transaction. Once wives or husbands – and particularly children – come into the picture, you would be extremely unwise not to insure.

A mortgage protection policy is half a loaf. It is better than nothing, but it is hardly going to solve all the financial problems that are going to face a widow, particularly if she has young children to support.

The cheapest way to increase cover is to go for level term assurance; a policy where the sum assured does not decrease over the years but remains at the same amount. Table 31 gives some examples of rates. When you are working out your insurance needs, remember that you may have some insurance automatically included in your pension scheme.

If you are self-employed or do not belong to a company pension scheme at work, you should be able to get insurance at effectively cheaper rates than those shown below. This is because you can take out a policy under the self-employed pensions legislation, and get tax relief (at your marginal rate – i.e. 27 per cent or more) on the premiums. These policies are known as "Section 226a" policies in the trade – and if you are eligible, it is sensible to make use of this concession. Many life companies operate these schemes and an insurance broker could certainly

Table 31 Examples of level term assurance

Sex	Age next birthday	Sum assured £	Term (years)	Monthly premium £
M	25	25,000	25	2.58
M	30	25,000	25	3.50
F	30	25,000	25	2.67
M/F	35/33	25,000	25	8.33

Source: *Equitable Life*.

point you in the right direction. When the new personal pensions become available in 1988, these will offer the same facility.

If you have an endowment mortgage, you will be in the same position as someone taking out a repayment mortgage with a MPP; your mortgage debt is covered but that is all.

If you are taking out the mortgage on a joint basis, you have two choices. The first is a 'joint life, first death' policy, where the sum assured is paid out in the event of either of you dying before the end of the mortgage term. The second is to take the endowment policy out on a 'single life' basis – in other words, a policy that only pays up if the person named in the policy dies before the end of the term – but supplementing it with additional term assurance on the other person's life.

Take the example of a couple aged under 30, with two small children. While it certainly will not be easy for the husband to cope should his wife die, it probably will not give rise to as many financial problems as if it happened the other way round. So instead of opting for a joint life, first death policy, the couple can save a bit of money by putting the endowment policy in the wife's name alone (this is because life assurance is cheaper for the female of the species as she tends to live longer). The monthly premium for a £25,000 endowment policy over 25 years would be £34.58 on the joint basis, but £33.42 on her life alone. The man could then take out a much higher term assurance policy on his own life, to make sure his widow would have enough not just to pay off the mortgage, but to make ends meet until she is able to go back to work again.

Another situation where it could be worth taking out the endowment policy solely in one person's name is where there is a history of ill health. Let us take the example of a married couple in their mid-40s: the husband, let us suppose, suffered a heart attack a couple of years ago. Through his company pension scheme, he is already well insured. In this case, it might be worth organising the endowment policy solely on his wife's life, as it will mean the premiums will be considerably cheaper.

There is another type of joint life policy, called 'joint life, last survivor'. This pays out only on the second death during the term of the policy. There is not a lot of point to this (except in circumstances where a life policy is being used purely as a means for investment).

Term assurance policies are cheap, particularly for younger ages, as Table 31 shows. There are several variations on the basic policy which has been described above. In the first place, you do not have to choose a term of 25 years: our examples use this only because that is also the usual length of a mortgage. You can take out a term policy for anything from five years upwards. The shorter the term, the cheaper the premiums for a given sum assured – not surprising since you are less likely to die within the next five years than within the next 25.

There are also Family Income Benefit policies, which instead of handing over a lump sum to your heirs, pay them a guaranteed income for a set number of years. You can also opt for 'index-linked' policies, where both the sum assured and the premiums increase every year in line with inflation. There is one thing to remember, however, if you have had such a policy – or any insurance policy – since before 13 March 1984. This qualifies for life assurance premium relief, and will continue to do so only if you keep it as it is and do not 'enhance the benefits' by increasing the sum assured or premiums or extending the term.

An insurance broker should be able to advise you on the best policy or package of policies for your circumstances. It is also worth approaching banks, some of which offer a full broking service. There is nothing to stop you arranging it all yourself, of course, as long as you are prepared to put in time and effort.

MORTGAGE INSURANCE GUARANTEES

These were mentioned in Chapter 2. If you are borrowing a larger than usual amount, the building society will automatically take out a mortgage insurance guarantee to protect itself against the possibility of your defaulting.

Guarantees are required generally when you are borrowing in

excess of 75 or 80 per cent of the property's valuation. The cost is about 2.8 to 4.0 per cent of the extra amount borrowed (it varies from lender to lender). So, if you are looking to borrow 95 per cent on a £30,000 property where the lender's usual rule is 80 per cent, you will have to pay a premium of, for example, £135 for the guarantee – that is £4,500 times 3.0 per cent.

This sum can usually be added to the mortgage loan, but not if you are borrowing 100 per cent of the valuation already. In that case, you will simply have to pay it up front.

INSURANCE FOR STRUCTURAL DEFECTS

If you are buying a brand-new house, you are normally covered by a scheme operated by the National House Building Council, which lasts for 10 years. In the first two years after completion, any defects that appear have to be made good by the builders. For the next eight years you are covered for any loss caused by 'major damage consequent upon a defect in the structure'.

If you are buying an older house, there is no insurance policy available at present to cover you against structural defects; so the moral must be, make sure you have a proper survey before you buy.

INSURANCE AGAINST REDUNDANCY AND ILL HEALTH

It is possible to take out an insurance policy which will cover your mortgage payments if you are made redundant. The cost is normally around £4.80 per month for each £100 of mortgage payment, including any endowment premium. There is often a maximum limit of around £500 per month. The scheme may also cover those who have to give up working through an accident or ill health. The mortgage payments are not covered indefinitely: a time limit of two years is typical.

CHAPTER 11

IN THE FUTURE: MOVING ON

If you thought buying a property was a fairly arduous process, buying and selling can be even worse. Horror stories abound, of 'chains' breaking, of gazumping, and even of 'reverse gazumping' – the situation where a buyer waits until the last minute and then just before the exchange of contracts, knowing that the person who is selling to him is totally committed to the next stage and could not pull out at this point even if he wanted so, suggests that the price be £1,000 or whatever less.

Another nightmare can be the so-called 'contract races', where a seller provisionally accepts offers from two or three hopeful buyers and says, 'The first one to arrange mortgage finance and complete preliminary legal processes wins'.

The reasons for doing this are quite understandable, if not forgivable. Anyone who has had the experience of a buyer dropping out at the very last minute will probably be determined that next time he will never be so foolish as to take one person's word again but will hedge his bets by having a few understudies in case the most likely buyer lets him down.

The problem is that this puts a number of people to what could be quite considerable expense. Each one has to pay for the building society valuation and possibly a survey; each may have to find a deposit as a sign of good faith to put down with the estate agent (true, this is returnable if the sale does not go through, but it still has to be found in the first place); and each will be incurring legal fees.

Part of the problem lies in the fact that the wheels of finance, and the wheels of law, can turn slowly – sometimes agonisingly slowly. Even when everything runs smoothly and there is no general shortage of mortgage finance, it can be a number of months before exchange of contracts is reached. But until this stage (outside Scotland) either side can pull out with impunity; and the longer the period of waiting the greater the likelihood that something will go wrong.

My feeling is that buying and selling a property is a horrid enough business as it is, without all the characters involved starting to behave like some soap opera businessman-villain. The only thing to do is grit your teeth, keep your fingers crossed, and behave in the way you would like others to treat you. And if someone does let you down, and you are sure there was not a good reason for it, then my advice is that you write them the nastiest letter you can bring yourself to compose. Then, if they have a conscience, they might at least be deterred from behaving in such a fashion again.

TIMING YOUR SALE

Now down to practicalities. When you move, should you try to sell first or buy first? Opinions differ over this. Conventional wisdom says that in a rising market you should fix up your purchase first, and then put your house on the market. That way, you will benefit from the rise in prices over the next month or two until you arrange your sale.

Many people, however, like to get their sale arranged first, preferring the bird-in-the-hand approach. There is also the point that, if you are facing competition from other people for the property you want to buy, you may be more attractive to the vendor than someone who has yet to put his own place on the market.

I think the right answer depends on the particular property you have for sale. If there is a strong demand in your area for your type of property, you may be able to take the risk of arranging to buy first, and only then putting your property on the market.

Suppose, however, the price you are hoping to get for your property depends partly on some very individual characteristics, which require a particular sort of buyer to be attracted by it. Then you might have to wait some time for the right price, in which case you would be wise to arrange your sale first, before committing yourself to a purchase.

Near where I live, for example, is a suburb that is full of three-bedroom bungalows. It is a respectable place which always attracts a steady stream of buyers looking for a three-bedroom bungalow; in fact owning one of them is as near to having liquid assets as any property can be. Then again, many country areas have fine period houses which are a little too large for the average family. They seem, to a Londoner's eye, absurdly good value; yet they can take many months to sell. The owner of one of these could find himself paying an expensive bridging loan for an uncomfortably long time if he followed the procedure of buying first.

Do not forget, it works the other way as well; if you are buying a 'difficult to sell' property, you have an inbuilt negotiating lever over the price (unless the sellers have taken this advice and can afford to wait, as they have not committed themselves elsewhere!). And as for determining whether your house comes into the 'easy' or 'difficult' category, there is no need to gaze into a crystal ball. Ask any estate agent for his honest opinion, or better still, ask half a dozen of them.

Some owners, who must be the bane of estate agents' lives, keep their property more or less permanently for sale, at an unrealistically high price, just in case they attract an offer at that level.

Selling a house costs more money – almost inevitably. Unless you have a friend round the corner willing to make you an offer, you will have to tell the world that your property is for sale – which costs money whichever way you go about it. The most common way is through an estate agent.

USING AN ESTATE AGENT

Estate agents generally charge a percentage of the sale price of the property. This can differ according to the area you live in. London and the South-East are generally the most expensive, with agents charging between 1½ per cent and 3 per cent of the price. If you give them 'sole agency' – that is, agree that you will instruct no other agency on the property – then they may charge 2 per cent (plus VAT). If you instruct several agents, the commission has to be shared between them, and so is likely to be a half per cent extra plus VAT.

Provincial estate agents may be a half per cent cheaper in both cases. If you are selling the ancestral home, however, you may find an agent charges 3 per cent or more.

Competition has been creeping into the estate agents' field as well as everything else, and you may find some who are prepared to negotiate on price. According to one London-based solicitor, who has plenty of experience of domestic conveyancing, estate agents' fees can now be anything between 1 per cent and 5 per cent, depending on the type of property and the amount of work they are prepared to do. It has to be good news for the seller, though it does mean that opportunities to save money are only there if you are prepared to use your rights as a consumer – in other words, to telephone round for estimates, to negotiate, and to strike a hard bargain.

SOLE AGENCY OR JOINT AGENCY?

Since the first action of most flat or house-hunters is to put themselves on every relevant estate agent's list, there does not seem a lot of point in instructing more than one agent – at least to begin with. If you have several weeks or months with no success, you might consider changing agents rather than adding another.

You should also have a rethink as to whether the price you are asking is actually realistic or whether the estate agent has persuaded you to pitch it at too high a level. Since agents are rewarded through a percentage of the selling price, it is in their interest to arrange a sale at as high a price as possible, and so this may lead them to suggest an unrealistically high figure. To balance that, however, it is also in their interest to sell the place as quickly as possible, as they do not get their fee until the sale is completed.

A sole agency seems the most sensible way of selling your house if you decide to use an estate agent. You should make clear to the agent, however, that you are not awarding them sole selling rights. If you did, this would mean that if you finally arranged a private sale, you would still have to pay the agent's fee.

Other aspects to make clear with the agent are, who pays for what in the selling process: the 'For Sale' board outside your door, for example, and any advertising. The normal practice seems to be that the board comes as part of the package, as does any small advertising suggested by the agent themselves. If you ask them to advertise the property, however, or large advertisements are proposed, they are likely to charge you for these services. They should, of course, consult you before any major additional expenditure is undertaken on your behalf.

While on the subject of sale boards, you do have a choice as to whether to have one up outside your home. I think it is a good idea. Plenty of people choose the area they want to live in first – and then drive round it looking at the sale boards. But one is enough – there is nothing that smacks of desperation so much as four or five sale boards lined up outside one house.

Estate agents normally belong to one or more professional bodies: the Royal Institution of Chartered Surveyors, the Incorporated Society of Valuers and Auctioneers or the National Association of Estate Agents. Using a member of one of these bodies means you will be protected should your estate agent run off with your deposit.

The situation in Scotland is different, as solicitors also act as estate agents there. Their fees for selling property are a maximum of 1.5 per cent, though if you are also using the same firm for conveyancing, you should be able to get a reduction. Solicitors in the rest of the country could be about to take on estate agents at their own game as the Law Society has recently given permission for them to set up their own property shops. How these will work, and what fees they will charge, remain to be seen.

ALTERNATIVES

DOING IT YOURSELF

If you decide to sell your property yourself, the heaviest cost you will have to bear is advertising. For the reasons given above, it is a good idea to put up your own 'For Sale' board. If you have one professionally done (look under 'Sign Makers' in the Yellow Pages) it could cost you between £40 and £70 depending on whether it is single- or double-sided. The board need only say 'House for Sale' and 'Apply within' if someone is likely to be in the house most days, or a telephone number if not.

Then you must decide where to advertise. You can start with cards in newsagents' windows, but apart from this you will have basically three alternatives: a local paper, a national paper and/or specialist papers. There are a growing number of 'freesheets' distributed in local areas, which often have large property sections which might be worth considering.

When you advertise in a newspaper, it is a better idea not to do so on a day when there are a large number of property advertisements. Yours will be sandwiched between scores of others. Instead choose a day where you will make a splash by being the only property advertisement in the whole issue.

The classified advertisement team at a newspaper will often offer advice as to what the advertisement should contain. 'Work from the top downwards' is one rule: start with area, the type of house (detached, semi-detached or terraced) the age, and then go into details of the number of bedrooms, reception rooms and so on. End with the price and your telephone number.

As far as the actual wording goes, there are a number of abbreviations which it is quite acceptable to use. 'Kit' and 'bath' are fine – k. and b. will do at a pinch. 'Fitted kit' sounds much better if you can afford the extra. Gas CH (central heating), F-hold (freehold) Gdn (garden) – we are all used to this type of shorthand, though there does come a point where too many abbreviations become difficult to read – let alone the fact that such an advertisement is unlikely to look enticing. Who is interested in a place that boasts: '1 R, 2B, K & B, Lg Lse, CH £30,000 ono'?

Since all house prices are understood to be negotiable, there is little point in including 'or offer' or 'or near offer' in the advertisement – it merely signals the fact that even you think it is probably overpriced! If you are desperate to sell, a better way of doing it is to state a price 'for quick sale' implying thereby that you have already reduced the price from what it could have fetched, if you had had the time to wait for the right buyer.

If you can afford it, put some extra detail into the advertisement other than the bare bones of the accommodation. Fully-fitted carpets for example; the size of the major rooms; the size of the garden. Do not be reluctant to point out all the good features while ignoring some of the bad. Remember, the purpose of the advertisement is to entice potential buyers to come and see the place, and it will be competing with perhaps dozens of other properties, some of them described by estate agents who, as we all know, are adept at making an ordinary house sound marvellous, and the awful appear adequate!

Finally, if you possibly can, put your telephone number (day and evening) in the advertisement. Most people hate writing to box numbers. As an illustration, consider the following two advertisements – I know which one would catch my eye, and which one would simply be passed over.

'£85,000 o.n.o. 3b. 2r. hse, gge. London SE25. Box no 1234'

or 'SE25, 10 mins. City. Unique 1890 det. hse, orig. features, 3 beds (2 dble) 2 recept (one 25' long) conservatory, Fitted kit, utility rm, bath. 60' x 70' gdn. Gas CH. Dbl gge. £85,000. 01-000 0000 (day) 000 0000 (eve).'

Not only does the second advertisement sound much more appealing, it actually makes the place look better value as well!

Of course, there is no such thing as the perfectly worded advertisement which is guaranteed to sell a property at the asking price. Most of it boils down to common sense – and how much you can afford to pay in lineage. Remember also to bear in mind the audience your advertisement is going to reach. There is little point in being very specific about location ('on the Waverly Estate') if your readers are drawn from a wide area like the whole of London. Or again, commuting time might be essential in the case of a lesser known London suburb, but could be meaningless for a small market town.

Most newspapers offer three styles of advertisement. In ascending order of cost, they are: lineage; semi-display; display. The difference between the last two is that semi-display has two lines above and below the advertisement; 'full display' is neatly boxed.

The advertising people will always suggest that you go for the full display; it makes the advertisement stand out, they say, therefore more people read it. My experience has in fact been the opposite: my flat was advertised, via an estate agent, in a national newspaper in a fairly prominent box with the estate agent's name emblazoned across the top. Yet when people rang up to enquire about it, several of them said 'You are selling privately, aren't you?'. In other words, they had absolutely no recollection of the form of the advertisement, only the content.

As to whether you have a photograph of your property along with the advertisement this really depends on where you advertise. Some local papers have photographs with every single advertisement (which can often mean pages with row upon row of murky pictures of 1930s semi-detached houses), and however pointless it might seem, your advertisement would look rather odd without one and people might suspect you had something to hide. Other papers, however, very rarely have photographs so in that case you do not need to bother.

As regards the price that you pitch your property at, an estate agent will actually do the work for you – and probably for nothing. The general rule is that estate agents will value a property with no obligation on your part to place it with them. They are understandably not enthusiastic about this – but they will do it.

Once you find a buyer for your property, the other thing you will have to do is to extract a deposit from them equivalent to the deposit that estate agents accept from buyers as a sign of good faith. Do not expect the buyer to be happy about handing the money over to you; you could ask for it to be held by your solicitor, if you are using one, or you could open a joint bank account with your buyer.

COMPUTER AGENCIES AND PROPERTY SHOPS

The other option is to use one of the new forms of selling property that have come into being in the last few years – computer agencies and property shops. Both are limited to certain parts of the country; both should work out cheaper than using an estate agent.

Computer agencies are not particularly suitable if you are selling from a distance, as they leave it up to you to make arrangements to see potential purchasers and show them round. The other disadvantage is that you are paying money in advance of a sale which might not materialise. If you are successful, however, you will be saving several hundreds of pounds. A £30,000 house, for example, could cost £400 or more to sell through an estate agent, compared to about £100 through a computer agency.

Property shops are to estate agents what a hypermarket is to the local delicatessen. Like the computer agencies, they charge a flat fee, payable in advance, which ranges from around £50 to £120 depending on the area. Property shops are more widely spread throughout the country than computer agencies although, again, they seem to be concentrated more in the southern half of the country than in the North.

The essential difference between both these alternatives and estate agents is that the latter act as your agent – they will advise you on what price to ask and whether to accept a lower offer, they will show prospective purchasers round your house, if necessary, and so on. With property shops and computer agencies, however, you are selling the property; although some may, to a greater or lesser extent, be prepared to offer advice, their main function is simply to provide you with the means to make the sale.

SELLING BY AUCTION

Property that is sold by auction tends to fall into one of the following categories.

1 'Investment' property, usually meaning either very large, old, run-down property more suitable for purchase by a firm of builders, or full or partially tenanted property.

2 Property sold by the trustees of an estate, where the trustees are under an obligation to demonstrate that they have sold the property at a proper market price (and auctions are the best way of establishing this).

3 Extremely unusual and/or expensive property where an estate agent would have difficulty in establishing an asking price.

The average owner-occupied home is unlikely to be suitable for selling by this means simply because the average buyer would not consider buying at auction. Its main advantage is speed.

If you are interested in buying at auction remember that the contract is established as soon as you have made a successful bid; so all the preliminary work and expenses (having a survey, establishing title, arranging a mortgage) has to be done beforehand, when you do not even know if you will succeed in getting the property. Although the risk of trying to buy at auction can be high, there could be one point in your favour; if you are bidding for a run-down property, remember that most of the competitive bidders are likely to be builders, who are looking for a quick profit from their work, so they will be willing to pay substantially less for the place and you could end up with a genuine bargain.

SHOWING PEOPLE ROUND

Whichever method of selling you use, it is likely that you will be responsible for showing prospective buyers round your house. Most people evolve a routine for this. Running costs are a subject brought up by most viewers, so have your answers prepared. Which rooms get the sun at which time of day is another favourite question. Work out in advance which fixtures and fittings are included in the purchase price and which ones (carpets and curtains, for example) you want extra money for.

Should you redecorate your house before you put it on the market? One gambit which has been suggested is that you slap on a fresh coat of white paint over the walls. My view is that as long as the place is clean, tidy and does not smell – and is in a reasonable state of decoration – then this is all that is required. Nearly everyone has a bit of the homemaker in them and once they start thinking 'all I have to do is paint that wall purple and that wall pink and the place will look marvellous', you are well on the way to making a sale. Present them with perfection, on the other hand, and there are no interesting possibilities.

Most serious viewers will probably want to have a look round the place on their own, once you have completed your guided tour. So make sure you shove the odd bits of jewellery out of sight and preferably locked away.

If you are going to come to a decision about a buyer face to face rather than directing it all through an estate agent, do not be reluctant to ask them questions about their finances. Have they sold their property yet? Are they part of a 'chain'? Have they got a reasonably firm source of mortgage finance? Work out a 'stalling' answer in advance so that if you begin to have doubts about someone as you are talking to them, you can deal with the situation smoothly.

THE MOVE

STAGE ONE

Once you have successfully found a buyer for your property and another place to buy, and assuming that nothing slips from cup to lip, you will be ready to move. You will, of course, have sorted out very precisely with your buyer and seller what you are respectively leaving and getting in the two properties.

Then you must decide whether to use a professional firm of removers to do the job for you – in which case you must ask for several estimates – or whether to cajole or entice friends and relations to help you to do it yourself, with undefined threats or offers of drinks.

STAGE TWO

The second stage, which is in my experience utterly inevitable, is deep despair and panic when you realise that you have accumulated at least twice as much stuff as you thought possible, and cannot work out how you will ever move it all.

STAGE THREE

There are a large number of letters to be written to the local council, Post Office, British Telecom and utilities – gas, electricity and water boards – to let them know the date you are leaving and where to, and people to see – milkman, newsagent, etc. – to cancel your regular orders.

It is important to get these chores done, as British Telecom, for example, have an unfortunate habit of cutting off a telephone if you do not let them know in good time who is taking over from you.

STAGE FOUR

On the day that you actually move, my advice is that you pack one box with the essentials that you are going to need in the next 12 hours. Of course, you run the risk of getting an uncomfortably clear insight into your real character that way – but it is worth it. My list would include towels, soap, tea and coffee, plates and cups, glasses and a bottle of wine.

When you want a break from the dreary process of unpacking – which you are going to – you have got everything you need without having to run between the boxes labelled 'Kitchen' and those labelled 'Bathroom' or 'Linen' or whatever.

MOVING WITH CHILDREN AND ANIMALS

If you are moving with children, try to get a friendly neighbour to provide you – and them – with supper the day before, and breakfast on the moving day itself. That way, you can run down the stocks of food in your old house, and concentrate on the move itself.

It is a good idea for young children to have their own special case which they are responsible for. They can decide which of their favourite toys to take with them on the journey, and by being 'in charge' of their own packing, they might be persuaded not to 'help' you too much!

If you are going to arrive at your new house late in the day, do make sure you have got some instant food for hungry young appetites, items which do not require cooking or unpacking the kitchen utensils. And do take torches, a bath plug and a supply of light bulbs with you – you would be surprised how many people take the light bulbs away when they move.

Strong dustbin liners – one for each child – are ideal for packing up the pyjamas and possibly clothes for the next day. You will then be able to get them to bed – and up the next morning – without having the finish the major unpacking that evening.

If you are moving with animals as well as children, the move can become a major military operation. The RSPCA can provide cheap cardboard travelling boxes for cats.

CHAPTER 12

STAYING PUT AND IMPROVING

Moving, even within fairly modest price ranges, is likely to add up to a fair sum: probably in the region of £2,000 to £3,000 (or more) if you are making a move in the £30,000 to £50,000 bracket. It is not surprising that taking this expense into account many people choose instead simply to stay put and improve their existing place – saving the moving fees and devoting the cash to installing central heating, for example. Major improvements like adding a third-storey in the loft or building an extension at ground level will probably require approval from the requisite authorities and outside finance.

PLANNING PERMISSION

The Department of the Environment produce a useful leaflet called *Planning Permission: A Guide for Householders*, which should probably be your first reading matter. The ground-rules, roughly speaking, are as follows:

1 If you are contemplating an extension (including garages), anything that adds more than 15 per cent to the building's existing volume (10 per cent in the case of terraced houses) requires planning permission. If the extension is over 4 metres high, or within 2 metres of an existing boundary, planning permission is required whatever the size.
2 New external walls must conform to thermal insulation and fire resistance standards laid down by the Building Regulations.
3 All new rooms must have a ceiling height of at least 7 feet 7 inches and ventilation (e.g. an opening window) equal in area to at least 5 per cent of the new floor area.
4 New floors should have a damp-proof course, and new drainage work must conform to the Building Regulations.

Loft conversions are unlikely to need planning permission (unless they are large enough to come under rule 1 above). If you have a ground-floor extension which is visible from the front of the house, you will have to seek permission. It is likely that the planners will require it to be in a style to match the current building. If you live in a conservation area, you will probably face even tougher rules on what you can and cannot do. And if you own a listed building then the rules become very strict indeed.

FINANCING THE IMPROVEMENTS

For major improvements, you are likely to need finance from an outside source. The good news is that it is likely to qualify for tax relief, as long as you keep within the £30,000 limit overall.

The bad news is that it may cost you more than the straightforward mortgage you took out to buy the property in the first place.

TAX RELIEF

Table 32 shows examples of the type of work which will qualify for tax relief on the interest of loans taken out to finance it.

Sometimes the rules are not that easy to interpret – and they can seem unfair. For example, if you had the bad luck to inherit an antedeluvian system of radiators and a clanking, clapped-out boiler and plan to install a new central heating system that works, then in theory this is a repair, not an improvement. According to the letter of the law, it will not qualify for tax relief. Your only hope is to tell all to your Inspector of Taxes and plead for clemency.

The limit on loans where the interest qualifies for tax relief does not increase if you take out additional loans for improvements: you are entitled to only £30,000 in all. If you have already used this up in connection with your house purchase, you will not have any left over and you will have to pay the gross interest rate on any loan used for home improvement.

In this respect, a repayment mortgage scores over the endowment version where the loan remains outstanding in full for the whole of the mortgage term, so that if you have taken out a £30,000 mortgage you have no chance of getting any more tax relief until you have seen it out. On the other hand, endowment mortgages can be useful by providing another means of finance. Of course, the limit on tax relief may be raised some time in the future, but in the short term the omens are not that good.

Now that the MIRAS system of collecting tax relief has come into operation, prospective borrowers have to sign a form declaring that the advance being made to them is for a purpose

Table 32 Tax relief and home improvements

---

1 Examples of improvements that will qualify for tax relief:

(a) Home extensions and loft conversions;

(b) Central and solar heating installations (excluding portable radiators and night storage radiators not fixed to a permanent spur outlet). The cost of replacing one form of heating with another, for example changing from oil to gas central heating, is included;

(c) Installations of double-glazing even though it is in a detachable form. Replacement of windows or doors generally is included;

(d) Insulation of roof or walls;

(e) Installation of bathrooms and other similar plumbing;

(f) Kitchen and bedroom units (for example sink units) which are affixed to and become part of the building. In practice a range of matching units may be treated as qualifying as a whole even though only some of them qualify (but always excluding cookers, refrigerators and similar appliances);

(g) Connection to main drainage;

(h) Erection and cost of garages, garden sheds, greenhouses, patios and fences;

(i) Recovering or reconstructing a roof;

(j) Construction or landscaping of gardens;

(k) Construction of swimming pools;

(l) Reconstruction of property e.g. conversion into flats;

(m) Underpinning of a house;

(n) Rebuilding a facade;

(o) Insertion or renewal of damp-proof course. Dry and wet rot treatment;

(p) Replacement of electrical installations;

(q) Extensive repointing, pebble-dashing, texture coating or stone cladding (but excluding painting);

(r) Installation of fire or burglar alarms;

(s) Installation of water softening equipment forming a permanent part of the plumbing system;

(t) Construction of driveways and paths;

(u) Extensive replacement of guttering;

The above list is not exhaustive. In particular, expenditure on a number of smaller items may be met by a combined loan qualifying for relief, e.g. improvements under the Clean Air Act, fire precaution works, installation of water heating and ring mains electricity and the concreting or other improvements of driveways or paths.

Because relief may not be available in every case in these categories, depending on the precise nature and extent of the works, an individual who is contemplating such expenditure and who would regard tax relief as an essential requirement, should contact his Inspector of Taxes for advice before entering into any commitment.

which will qualify for tax relief under existing legislation. If you make a false declaration which is found out at a later date, it counts as tax evasion and you will be dealt with severely by the Revenue.

However, there is nothing to stop you maximising the amount you borrow to carry out improvements on your home so that you can use your spare cash for things that do not qualify for tax relief. If you decide to build a garage and buy a car, for example, and you have got enough money saved to buy one of these outright, make sure it is the car, as the garage will qualify for tax relief on the interest, the car will not.

WHERE TO FIND FINANCE

BUILDING SOCIETIES AND BANKS

Your first port of call for the extra money you need should be the building society or bank with whom you have your mortgage. In the last few years, the number of 'further advances' made by building societies has been running at around 10 per cent of their total number of loans. As an alternative ask your bank for a loan, or try a top-up from an insurance company.

THE COST

You may have to pay for another valuation on your property, while there could be an arrangement fee – anything between £20 and £100 – as well. The practice varies quite widely between different lenders. Bearing this in mind, the minimum further advance it is worth going for is £1,000 or so.

THE INTEREST RATE

Some societies charge the same rate for further advances as they do for their basic mortgage. Others charge a differential rate or series of rates, depending on the nature of the improvements to be made. Although another society might have cheaper loans than your current one, you cannot get a further advance from one who is not lending on your main mortgage – you would have to switch the whole lot to the new one.

If you have an endowment mortgage (or an endowment or whole life policy which is not linked to a house purchase scheme) then you may be able to get a loan from the insurance company concerned. The company may want you to take out an additional policy – particularly if the first one is linked to your mortgage. Try to avoid 'non-profit' policies: they are as gloomy as they sound. What they do is guarantee to pay off the loan at the end of the term (or earlier if you die in the meantime) but there is never any surplus for you. So effectively, whatever the interest rate says it is, it is more: loans linked to non-profit policies are an expensive way of borrowing money.

If you approach a lender other than the one you have for your main mortgage, they will also want some security for the loan. You will have to get your original lender's permission for this, but there is usually no problem, assuming you have built up enough equity of your own in the property. There may be a fee for registering the second lender's interest in the place, of £23 plus solicitor's costs.

THE TERM OF THE LOAN

If you are borrowing from your bank or building society, the term of the further advance is usually set to coincide with the original mortgage term. Sometimes you can re-schedule the total amount borrowed over a fresh 25 years, particularly if the additional loan is large in relation to the total.

INTEREST-ONLY LOANS FOR RETIRED HOME-OWNERS

Some societies, such as the Halifax, Anglia and Northern Rock, offer interest-only home improvement loans to elderly people. The capital does not have to be paid back until the property is sold, which means the monthly payments in the meantime are relatively low. You could also find that the Department of Health and Social Security will help out with these payments.

LOCAL AUTHORITY GRANTS

You may be lucky and find that your local authority is still making grants available for the improvement of privately-owned homes. The present system is described in a booklet called *Home Improvement Grants* published by the Department of the Environment and available from your local authority or Citizens Advice Bureau. However, as many councils have now run out of money these grants are scarce; the whole system is currently under review.

One point you have to bear in mind with any improvement is that you should inform your local authority of it once it has been completed. It is likely to increase your home's rateable value, which means unfortunately that your rates bill will inevitably rise.

ARE HOME IMPROVEMENTS A GOOD INVESTMENT?

The first rule of looking after your property is to make sure that it is wind proof and watertight. A beautiful fitted bathroom matters little if you cannot take baths when it is raining, thanks to the leaking roof.

If you are planning to stay in your house for the next 20 years or so, it does not really matter what sort of improvements you make; they will be for your own use, and you can ignore whether their cost will be reflected in the selling price.

For home-owners who have a shorter term view however, it is worth bearing in mind what improvements will help to sell your house, which ones are neutral, and which have a positively harmful effect. Top of the list, in terms of 'adding value' come fitted kitchens and bathrooms, fitted wardrobes, central heating and garages, particularly where there is enough space to have a 'utility' area, or a work bench. Installing double glazing does not appear to be a great selling point; it simply does not appeal to many people, and in terms of the savings you will make on fuel bills from having it installed, it will be a very long time before you recoup the cost of installation. Loft and cavity wall insulation are not great selling points either, although the former is efficient in saving on heating, given that it does not cost too much to install in the first instance.

One point you should bear in mind is that it is possible to 'over-improve' your house. Estate agents say that you should be wary of having the most expensive house in your street. Since property prices are probably determined more by position than by any other factor, buyers will simply not pay more than a certain amount for a property in that area, however many 'mod cons' it may have attached to it. For this reason, house extensions such as a sun lounge may prove a bad investment because you might be unable to get back anything like its cost. Loft extensions, however, seem to be the exception to the rule: if you can pack in a fourth bedroom under the roof, it could well pay off.

CHAPTER 13

THE PROBLEM CHAPTER

There are all sorts of problems connected with house owning, but some of them you can prepare for and some, with a bit of luck, may pass you by. In this chapter we look at the most common difficulties likely to confront house-buyers and what you can do about them.

GETTING A MORTGAGE AND COMPLETING THE SALE

1 YOUR BUILDING SOCIETY OR BANK WILL NOT LEND YOU ENOUGH.

If this is because your income does not match up to their requirements, you can try another lender who might have more generous rules in this respect. At the time of writing, most building societies and banks are prepared to lend up to three times income. The Halifax has a special scheme for first-time buyers enabling them to borrow up to three and three-quarter times their income as long as they have saved a sufficient deposit.

Some of the smaller societies may also be more lenient in this respect, but beware of taking on a mortgage at an extra high interest rate just because someone is willing to lend you the money. You will be stretched as it is borrowing three times your income, and at today's relatively high interest rates it could spell financial disaster. It is worth consulting a mortgage broker here, who may know of lenders prepared to stretch their usual rules, but at the basic mortgage rate.

If your problem is that the lender down-values your property, again you have several options:
(a) Go back to the seller and see if you can negotiate a reduction in the purchase price.
(b) Ask your building society or bank if they will lend you more, supported by a mortgage insurance guarantee for the extra.
(c) Try another lender. The drawback with this is that you will have to pay out a second valuation fee, and there is no guarantee that the second valuer will look on the property any more kindly than the first. But valuation is an art rather than a science, and you may be lucky.

If you are looking for 100 per cent of the purchase price, you may be able to arrange a special top-up mortgage with an insurance company where they are prepared to allow buyers to borrow up to 105 per cent of the valuation: a mortgage broker may be able to advise. Alternatively, you might be able to arrange a second mortgage on the property via a bank, which might last for 10 years rather than the customary 25 years of the first mortgage.

Be sure you really, really want the place before you go ahead on a scheme like this. There comes a point when it becomes more sensible simply to look for another property more within your price range.

2 YOU HAVE GOT THE MORTGAGE ARRANGED, BUT YOU DO NOT HAVE THE CASH FOR THE 10 PER CENT DEPOSIT.

The 10 per cent deposit is usually required (outside Scotland) about a month before completion, which is the time the lender actually makes the funds available. If you do not have the money for this – either because you are getting a 100 per cent mortgage on the property, or because it is tied up in the house you are selling, there are two courses of action to take.

(a) Ask your solicitor to negotiate a lower percentage for the deposit if possible. These days, particularly with highly priced property, it is common for deposits of 5 per cent rather than 10 per cent to be put down at this stage. The other side is not obliged to accept this – after all that 10 per cent is your seller's only comfort if you then pull out of the sale, leaving him high and dry (true, he can sue you for the balance but given the cost of legal fees and the time involved, he would be silly not to prefer as high a deposit as possible).

(b) If there is still a shortfall, your bank should be reasonably happy to lend you the balance. You may have to pay an arrangement fee, and the rate of interest will be quite high (3 to 4 per cent above bank base rate). This interest qualifies for tax relief (assuming the total borrowed is £30,000 or less) but the loan will not be under the MIRAS system and so you must tell the Revenue about it in order to get the relief. Alternatively, your building society may lend you this: it will be at.a higher rate than their normal mortgage rate and the bank may work out cheaper.

3 YOUR BUILDING SOCIETY WILL LEND YOU THE MONEY YOU NEED BUT ONLY AFTER YOU HAVE CARRIED OUT CERTAIN SPECIFIED REPAIRS OR IMPROVEMENTS.

There may be no problem here: builders should not in general be paid until after completion of the work, at which point the money from the building society will be available.

However, if the society will not even lend you enough to purchase the place until the repairs have been carried out, you will have to go back to your bank manager.

One tip here: if you are buying a property which requires some (non-urgent) repairs or improvements and you are contemplating going back to the society in a year or two for a further advance, do not: it is much better to see if you can borrow all the money to begin with, as you will not be charged the differential rate you might otherwise be if you went for the separate loan at a later stage. It could also mean that the whole lot qualifies for tax relief whereas if you went back later the tax office might disqualify part of it.

4 YOU ARE BUYING A NEW HOUSE AND THE BUILDERS WANT THE MONEY IN STAGES AS IT IS BEING BUILT.

Provided the builders are registered with the National House Building Council there should be no problems. The building society will release the money in stages as required.

The society may, however, require their valuer to visit the site to inspect progress, and the fee for this is likely to be added to your mortgage.

If you want to buy a house that is not being built by an NHBC builder, it is important that you speak to the building society first, as some are not necessarily willing to lend on this basis.

5 YOU HAVE FOUND A PLACE TO BUY, BUT AT THE LAST MINUTE THE PERSON WHO HAD ARRANGED TO BUY YOURS DROPS OUT.

You have three options here. You can try to hold up the chain of buyers and sellers, to allow you time to find a new buyer; you can withdraw from the proposed purchase; or, if you are determined to go ahead, you will have to ask your bank manager for a bridging loan.

Tell your building society at once about the situation, if you still want to go ahead. They may be willing to let you continue with your old mortgage for the time being as well as taking on the fresh one; this you should do, as it is a cheap form of borrowing, and (assuming the loan is under £30,000) you will be paying it net of tax relief which can be important simply from a cash-flow point of view.

Under the tax rules, you will qualify for tax relief on a bridging loan up to £30,000 in addition to a new mortgage of the same amount, for up to one year.

For the rest of the money you need to borrow, the bank manager is the main option. They do not like 'open-ended bridging' as they call it, simply because they do not know when you will be in a position to pay them back. You will probably have an interview with your bank manager. Go to him with every single bit of relevant information: the size of your existing mortgage, the size of the new one, the amount of capital that is locked up in your existing property, the price you are asking for it, whether you have received any initial offers for it and so on.

He may ask for a second charge on one or other of the properties, for which you will have to get the building society's permission, though this should not present a problem. Remember you must inform your tax office of the amount of interest you are paying in order to get the tax relief, as you will be paying the interest gross.

OFF AND RUNNING: PROBLEMS IN THE MIDDLE OF A MORTGAGE

1 THE MORTGAGE INTEREST RATE GOES UP AND YOU ARE HAVING DIFFICULTY MEETING THE INCREASED LEVEL OF MORTGAGE PAYMENTS.

If you have a repayment mortgage, you can apply to the lender to extend the term of your mortgage, which will keep the payments down. In exceptional circumstances, they might allow you to go on to an interest-only basis for a short time, but only if there is evidence that your situation is going to improve in the near future. Normally they are not willing to see a loan extend to beyond your retirement age. With an endowment mortgage, no such option is open to you as you are only paying interest on the loan in any case.

2 YOU HAVE A MORTGAGE – BUT YOU ARE PAYING WAY OVER THE ODDS FOR IT.

It could be that at the time you took out your mortgage, they were difficult to come by, or you needed one that was especially lenient on the income criterion, with the result that you are paying 1 per cent or 2 per cent or even more over the current basic rates. If you are about to move house, you should make sure you change your lender at the same time and go for a more competitive one – there is usually no problem over that.

But suppose you do not want to move house, only your mortgage: is this possible? The answer is yes, at times when mortgage funds are in reasonable supply. Not all societies are keen to take in someone else's washing in this way, but some will, as will some of the banks.

A change of mortgage will cost money. You could have to pay for a further valuation fee; there will be legal fees involved in transferring the deeds from your old lender to the new one; there could also be an arrangement fee for the new mortgage. In addition, if you are using a mortgage broker to help you here, but are not taking out a fresh endowment policy, you could expect to pay a fee to them. The first three items could well cost in the region of £200 to £250: to work out whether the whole process is worth it to you, have a look at Table 11, page 61.

If you can save 2 per cent on the mortgage rate, the net monthly payment on a £30,000 mortgage works out nearly £30 a month cheaper, which means you will make a 'profit' after only eight months. With larger mortgages the saving is even greater as there is no helping hand with tax relief on the interest.

3 YOU HAVE BEEN MADE REDUNDANT.

If this – unhappily no long rare – occurrence should happen to you, tell your building society about it at once. You win no brownie points by keeping a stiff upper lip and maintaining silence – quite the reverse, in fact. It is worth telling them even if you anticipate no great difficulty in getting another job and do not expect to fall behind with your mortgage payments. Should things take a turn for the worse, it will stand you in good stead; and, if they are quickly resolved as you expect, it will not have done you any harm.

If you become unemployed, building societies will usually allow you to put your mortgage on to an interest-only basis (this applies only to repayment mortgages; endowment mortgages are interest-only in any case). You should apply to the DHSS for supplementary benefit immediately. It will pay your mortgage interest and rates for you (assuming the Department considers the amount 'reasonable' – i.e. your house is not too luxurious or otherwise inappropriate). The big drawback here, however, is that you are only eligible if your savings are under £3,000. And since January 1987, the DHSS will pay only *half* the mortgage interest during the first six months of unemployment; though if you are still unemployed at the end of that time, it picks up the whole bill thereafter.

If you simply stop making your mortgage payments and offer no explanation to your building society, they may begin to make moves to evict you: their alarm bells start ringing after you have missed two monthly mortgage payments without explanation. The process can be a lengthy one, with plenty of opportunity for the borrower to come to some sort of arrangement before the society takes court action to re-possess the house. Nevertheless, the number of cases has been rising: in the first half of 1984, societies took possession of 5,230 properties compared with 2,900 in the whole of 1982, and the upward trend has continued. The number of people obtaining supplementary benefit for mortgage interest has also been rising from 98,000 in 1979 to 235,000 in 1982.

If you are in considerable financial difficulties, you could consider 'trading down' as an alternative to waiting for your house to be re-possessed. However, with estate agents' and legal fees, it is likely to be an expensive business and you may not come out of the deal with as much as you had hoped. If the lender conducts a forced sale, they will charge their legal and other costs on the sale to you. In the case of a forced sale, the lender is under a statutory obligation to obtain the best price possible, and therefore you can sue if they fail to do so.

4 YOU HAVE TO GIVE UP WORK BECAUSE OF ILL HEALTH.

The same considerations apply here as when you are made redundant. You might be lucky enough to work for an employer who provides an effective sick-pay scheme, in which case your problems on the mortgage front should not be insurmountable. However, you may still find it necessary to request an interest-only mortgage for a time if the level of sick pay is considerably less than your normal salary. It is possible to take out an insurance policy to cover your mortgage payments in the event of being unable to work through ill health or redundancy. You should consult an insurance broker for details. The monthly cost is around £4.80 to £5.00 per £100 of mortgage payments per month.

THE SPECIAL PROBLEMS OF FLAT OWNERS

In England and Wales (though not in Scotland) flats are nearly always leasehold. Most building societies are in fact unwilling to lend on freehold flats in England and Wales because of problems over maintenance and squabbles about 'who should pay for what'.

Leasehold flats are not, however, necessarily a bed of roses. There are two main problems a leaseholder faces. Firstly, there may well be difficulties with the managing agents of the block, who may not be carrying out their duties properly according to the lease, or who are charging too much for what they do.

The second problem is that of a declining lease, which at some point will begin to affect its saleability and value. As leases approach cut-off point at 50 to 55 years a building society will refuse to lend on normal (25-year) mortgage terms.

Leaseholders in flats have two possible solutions to this problem which are discussed below, though both depend on the agreement of the freeholder, who is not obliged to help you (unlike the case of leasehold houses, where under the Leasehold Reform Act of 1967 leaseholders have the right to buy their freehold).

BUYING THE LEASE

The first option is to get the other leaseholders of your block together to buy the lease. The most sensible way of doing this is to form a limited company as the body that will actually hold the freehold and then grant yourselves as occupiers of the flats fresh, long leases.

The formation costs of the company are likely to be upwards of £150. Most firms of solicitors will undertake the job for you – some more or less specialise in this sort of business. The Memorandum and Articles of such a company have to be carefully written so that there are provisions, for example, for every leaseholder to have an equal share in the freehold. They should also compel leaseholders to sell their share when they sell their flat.

There will be other costs apart from those incurred in forming the company. The freehold has to be conveyed (more legal costs); the management accounts of the company have to be audited and annual returns produced (auditor's fees and a £20 charge for filing the annual returns); and, of course, there is the price of the freehold.

Freeholders will be looking for a sum large enough to compensate them for the loss of the annual ground rent: the size of the sum will partly depend on the level of interest rates at the time you are negotiating. Apart from this, at some point the capital value of the property will begin to make itself felt and the sum requested will rise accordingly. You may find it wise to employ a professional valuer, in which case his fees will have to be met as well.

EXTENDING THE LEASE

Buying the freehold does not, however, mean that all your problems are necessarily over – they could just be starting. The responsibilities of running the block will now be yours and your neighbours; and life could become unpleasant if they refuse to pay their share of the maintenance costs.

Another solution, which would circumvent these problems, is simply to negotiate an extension of the lease. Again, a valuer may be required to help you arrive at a fair price; but unfortunately there is nothing that can be done if your freeholder sticks out for a higher one.

A Private Member's Bill, aiming to give flat leaseholders the same rights as those of house leaseholders, failed to get through Parliament in 1982. It is possible, however, that such legislation will be reintroduced in the near future. The Building Societies Association has produced a report recommending freehold flats on the Australian system of 'strata title' and the Lord Chancellor's department is currently investigating whether this sytem, or some other, would be more appropriate.

FINANCE

Whether you are seeking to buy the freehold or simply extend the lease, you may need outside finance to do so. In that case your building society will probably be willing to add the requisite amount to your mortgage.

SERVICE CHARGES IN FLATS

The lease should spell out in detail the service charges you will be faced with. The problem blocks of flats are those – often built in the 1930s – that have a communal heating and hot-water system, which can mean that the bills you face for this are astronomical, even though you use it very little. It can also, understandably enough, have an adverse effect on the value of your flat.

The Department of the Environment and Welsh Office provide a free booklet called *Service Charges in Flats* which sets out your rights under the Housing Act 1980. You may also find it useful to contact (and join) the Federation of Private Residents' Associations, a non-political, non-profit-making voluntary organisation which acts as a pressure group on behalf of both tenants and long leaseholders in flats.

NEARING THE END OF THE MORTGAGE TERM

It may not seem like it now, but one of these days you are going to get near the end of your mortgage term. If you have chosen a building society repayment mortgage, it is worth remembering that the effective net rate of interest rises markedly in the last couple of years and so it will be in your interest to pay it off early.

When you do so, however, ask your building society manager if you can leave a nominal sum – £10 or so – outstanding. That way, you can continue to have the deeds stored at their expense, not yours, and it will make the way easier should you ever wish to go back for a further mortgage for improvements at a later date.

Finally, it cannot be emphasised enough that, if you have problems with your mortgage, you should let your lender know. A financial problem shared is not always a problem halved – but it could be a vital step towards it.

SOURCES OF FURTHER INFORMATION

If you know where to look and whom to talk to, there is an enormous amount of information available (often free of charge) to the public on matters connected with house-buying, mortgages, insurance and so on. Below is a list of some of the organisations who may be worth contacting.

General information on house purchase and mortgages
The Building Societies Association
3 Savile Row
London W1X 1AF
01-437 0655
Publishes a booklet, *Building Societies and House Purchase*, and two leaflets, *Hints for Home Buyers* and *Taxation and the Building Society Borrower*, all of which are free.
    Practically all individual building societies issue their own literature, including booklets on home improvements, decorating and insulation among other topics – take your pick at the various branches near you.

General information on mortgage interest rates
Blay's Mortgage Tables (updated monthly) published by:
Blay's Guides Ltd
Churchfield Road
Chalfont St Peter SL9 9EQ
Should be available in local libraries.

General information on home insurance
The Association of British Insurers
Aldermary House
10-15 Queen Street
London EC4N 1TU
01-248 4477
Publishes a series of leaflets on home and other types of insurance.

Mortgages and insurance brokers
If you need a broker, contact one of the organisations below:
Corporation of Insurance and Finance Advisors
6 Leapdale Road
Guildford
Surrey
(0438) 35786

British Insurance Brokers' Association
BIBA House
14 Bevis Marks
London EC3
01-623 9043

Organisations offering index-linked mortgages
Index Linked Mortgage and Investment Company Ltd
Victoria House
178-180 Fleet Road
Fleet GU13 8SD
(02514) 29191

The Building Trust
25-26 Albemarle Street
London W1X 4AD
01-493 9899

New houses
National House Building Council
58 Portland Place
London W1N 4BU
01-637 1248

House Building Advisory Bureau
10 Bolt Court
London EC4
01-583 0518
Free booklets available on house purchase and new house construction methods.

The legal side
The Law Society
113 Chancery Lane
London WC2A 1PL
01-242 1222

The Law Society of Scotland
PO Box 75
26 Drumsheugh Gardens
Edinburgh EH3 7YR
031-226 7411
Will give you a list of solicitors' firms in your area.

The National Association of Conveyancers
2-4 Chichester Rents
Chancery Lane
London WC2A 1EJ
01-405 8582

Estate agents, surveyors and valuers
National Association of Estate Agents
Arbon House
21 Jury Street
Warwick CV34 4EH
(0926) 496800

The Royal Institution of Chartered Surveyors
12 Great George Street
Parliament Square
London SW1P 3AD
01-222 7000

The Incorporated Society of Valuers and Auctioneers
3 Cadogan Gate
London SW1X 0AS
01-235 2282

Moving
British Association of Removers
279 Gray's Inn Road
London WC1X 8SY
01-837 3088
Will provide a list of members in your area; publishes a number of free leaflets
on moving.

Home improving, building and decorating
Royal Institute of British Architects
66 Portland Place
London W1N 4AD
01-580 5533

Royal Incorporation of Architects in Scotland
15 Rutland Square
Edinburgh EH1 2BE
031-229 7205

Architectural Association
34-36 Bedford Square
London WC1B 3FS
01-636 0974

Architects' Registration Council of the United Kingdom
73 Hallam Street
London W1N 6EE
01-580 5861

National Home Improvement Council
26 Store Street
London WC1E 7BT
01-636 2562

National Association of Building Centres
26 Store Street
London WC1E 7BT
01-637 8361
Provides an information service and permanent exhibitions on building products, materials and services for trade and public.

Association of Manufacturers of Domestic Electrical Appliances (AMDEA)
AMDEA House
593 Hitchin Road
Stopsley
Luton LU2 7UN
(0582) 412444

Builders's Merchants' Federation
15 Soho Square
London W1V 5FB
01-493 1753

Cement and Concrete Association
Wrexham Springs
Slough SL3 6PL
(028 16)2727
Provides various leaflets on the use of concrete in the home and garden improvement projects. Details available in free catalogue.

Council of British Ceramic Sanitaryware Manufacturers
Federation House
Station Road
Stoke-on-Trent ST4 2RT
(0782) 48675
Issues free booklets on bathrooms and *Why a Bidet?*

Federation of Master Builders
33 John Street
London WC1N 2BB
01-242 7583
Provides a list of builder members to the public.

Fibre Building Board Development Organisation (FIDOR)
1 Hanworth Road
Feltham TW13 5AF
01-751 6107
Free publications and advice available on use of insulating and hardboard.

Glass and Glazing Federation
6 Mount Row
London W1Y 6DY
01-409 0545
Provides literature and information on all aspects of glazing.

Heating and Ventilating Contractors' Association
ESCA House
34 Palace Court
Bayswater
London W2 4JG
01-229 5543

Institute of Plumbing
Scottish Mutual House
North Street
Hornchurch RM11 1RU
(040 24) 51236
Issues list of registered plumbers.

National Association of Plumbing, Heating and Mechanical Services
Contractors
6 Gate Street
London WC2A 3HX
01-405 2678
Gives advice and information on plumbing and heating.

National Coal Board
Solid Fuel Advisory Service
Hobart House
Grosvenor Place
London SW1X 7AE
01-235 2020
Provides free advice and information on use of solid fuel.

National Fireplace Council
PO Box 35
Stoke-on-Trent ST4 7NU
(0782) 44311
Free catalogue available.

Publications
For surveys of past results and endowment policies, consult:

Money Management
Greystoke Place
Fetter Lane
London EC4A 1ND

Magazines on new houses, mortgages and other topics of general interest
connected with house purchase include:

Homebuyer
Haymarket Publishing Ltd
38–42 Hampton Road
Teddington TW11 0JE

What House
Parkway Publications Ltd.
315 Kilburn High Road
London NW6

What Mortgage
Financial Magazines Ltd
1st Floor
Consort House
26 Queensway
London W2

Miscellaneous
Consumers' Association
Subscription Department
Caxton Hill SG13 7LZ
01-839 1222
Publishes *Which?*, *Money Which?*, *Handyman Which?* and several books, e.g.
The Legal Side of Buying a House

Department of the Environment
Publications Stores
Building 3
Victoria Road
South Ruislip HA4 0NZ
01-845 7788
Publishes free leaflets on housing, including *Service Charges in flats: a guide for landlords and tenants* available from Citizens' Advice Bureaux and direct from above address.

If you live in Scotland, Wales or Northern Ireland, the Scottish Information Office, the Welsh Office and the Northern Ireland Housing Executive publish similar material.

Federation of Private Residents' Associations
11 Dartmouth Street
London SW1
01-222 0037

National Federation of Housing Associations
175 Gray's Inn Road
London WC1
01-278 6571
Central agency for housing associations.

INDEX